* * *

ESSENTIAL

[home repair]

a seasonal guide to maintaining your home

[contents]

FIRST EDITION
ISBN 0-9666753-3-9

10 9 8 7 6 5 4 3 2 1

COVER PHOTOGRAPHY:
KELLER & KELLER

Library of Congress Cataloging-in-Publication Data
This Old House essential home repair : a seasonal guide to maintaining your home.
    p.   cm.
    ISBN 0-9666753-3-9
    1. Dwellings—Maintenance and repair Amateurs' manuals.   I. This Old
House magazine.
TH4817.3. T46   1999   99-22949
643' .7—dc21   CIP

[introduction]

A HOME IS A PLACE OF REFUGE, A CASTLE, A SANCTUARY. A HOUSE, however, is a complex and immensely expensive mechanism that seems always in need of attention. In fact, a house is the single largest expense most of us will ever incur, reason enough to maintain it. And as master carpenter Norm Abram and contractor Tom Silva have learned in their decades of working on old houses, it's easier to tackle problems when they're small than to go after monsters nurtured by neglect. Ignored, a house will succumb to the ravages of time and weather. Maintained, it can last nearly forever. *** But where to start and what to do? Let Norm and Tom give you a hand. In the following chapters, drawn from the pages of *This Old House* magazine, they'll show you where to look for problems and explain what to do when you find them. Many ills—rotted siding, choked chimneys and overflowing gutters, for example—can be prevented by routine maintenance. Others, such as wobbling stair balusters, leaking basements and dead switches, call for deft repairs. In any case, peek over the shoulders of these craftsmen to see how they do it. Want to know the most common source of problems found in most houses? "On every house we've looked at in the years we've been doing this," says Norm, "most of the damage has been from water." Know your enemy: Read on.

—THE EDITORS

"WATER is a home's greatest ENEMY. ACCUMULATING IN THE basement, it can warp floorboards in rooms ABOVE AND TURN FINISHED ROOMS INTO MILDEWY CAVES UNFIT FOR habitation."

[lookingfortrouble]

NORM ABRAM PEERS STRAIGHT UP THE SIDE OF THE VERY WORN 19-room, three-bath Federal and gets set to give it a closer look. It's his first chance to inspect the season's project for *This Old House*, and he wants to know what the crew is in for. To figure that out, Norm insists on a proper inspection, one that begins with a "cruise around the outside." And it should be organized: "You start at the top and work down," says Norm.

Though Norm is inspecting someone else's house, he'd take the same approach with his own house. In fact, it's a good idea for every home owner to cruise around the outside—and wander through the basement—once or twice each year in order to locate small problems before they grow into monsters.

Staring up at the roof, Norm walks backward down Salem's historic Lynn Street until he gets a full house away, where he finally has a view of the ridgeline, almost 40 feet up. "I like to look at the roof and eave lines—these are nice and straight, not much sag—and I look for where the roof water is going to go: Can it cause ice dams in the winter?" He is impressed that the roof is slate, "but slate can crack and the shingles can slip. I see a lot of loose and broken shingles, and the ridge cap looks rough." He doesn't see any venting in the eaves. "Nothing ruins a roof faster than moisture in the attic."

Next Norm shifts his focus to the chimneys. "I look first to see if they're leaning—that's trouble—and then at their shape. Chimneys shouldn't have ledges that trap water and ice. This one is nice and straight." But then he looks harder and says, "Hmmm. I can see right through the spaces between the bricks—some of the mortar has deteriorated. The chimneys may need cleaning too." Working his way down visually, Norm stops at the gutter line.

The older a structure is, the more likely it is to need work; you won't know what it needs until you look. Only a thorough inspection can tell you what to expect. Here, Norm studies the Salem house.

[**looking for trouble**]

Steve and Richard (above) examine a plumbing nightmare: a jumble of pipes made of several different materials. Unsupported pipes can wobble as water moves through, and the weakened joints can leak.

The tip of a knife blade located rot at the base of this front-porch column.

The crown moldings where the roof meets the sides of this house are detailed and complicated, unlike anything he has seen on a Federal. He wonders if internal gutters are hidden there, then spies aluminum ones on other parts of the house and decides the gutters are just missing. "I don't think this house had gutters originally, so it would be nice to see it stay that way. The overhangs seem fine, and gutters look awful."

Sizing up the structure with his hand, he declares: "The house is square and straight." That means the windows are too, which is important because there are 58 of them. "The sashes appear to be closing straight, and the sills are sloped, so we won't see rot there because water can't collect. These windows are very, very old, though," he says, approaching a large bay on the side of the house. "They're single-pane—not very energy-efficient." The sash joints are also separated at the corners and need rebuilding. He suggests the windows be restored, not replaced. "We want to preserve the historic nature of the house."

Now bending down to waist level, Norm begins poking with his knife. He finds some rot in the wood panels under a bay window and some soft wood in the trimboard along the foundation. There's rot, too, in the sill plate at the front door and under one of the porch columns. The foundation is high off the ground and solid, much of it granite. "There should be little or no insect damage," he says. Dirt around the foundation should be at least 8 inches away from the siding to keep bugs and rot away. The brick sidewalk in front is pitched away from the house, which keeps water from running towards the

<< **It's a good idea** for every home owner to cruise around the house once or twice each year to locate small problems before they grow into monsters. >>

foundation—still, sidewalks should be checked every year because frost heave can easily nudge them out of place.

Down in the basement, Richard Trethewey is looking for other indicators of the house's health: "That's where the root of the tree is." Electrician Paul Kennedy Jr. is with him at the circuit-breaker box. "This doesn't look too bad," he says. "I'm bending the wires going into the box to see if they're flexible. That means they haven't overheated." Tracing wires from the box to joist-mounted junction boxes, he notes that the connections are taped solder joints. "Wire nuts are much better—solder joints can break—but I'd leave them alone unless they show signs of having heated up."

Richard takes a quarter and begins tapping the bottom of the cast-iron waste pipes. "If I hear a clear ringing, everything is okay. If the sound goes dead, that means the pipe is rotten." He quickly discovers a leaking drainpipe from a bathroom and under it a mishmash of water pipes with hurried solder connections. The plumbing is full of drum traps, devices—not allowed by current codes—that can't be snaked like the more modern P-style traps. "Nobody notices plumbing until it goes bad," he sighs.

Up on the roof, Steve checks loose and crumbling mortar atop a chimney on the oldest part of the house. A proper chimney cap would prevent water from infiltrating the brickwork and gradually destroying it. Down in the basement, the main circuit-breaker box is the first stop on any tour of a house's electrical system.

[bugdefense]

IN THE WARM MONTHS, A VISitor's first up-close impression of your house is often of its weakest part—a plain screen door. Flimsy, boring and creaky, the typical lumberyard offerings are hopelessly unimaginative and uninspiring. "Home owners," says architect Dennis Wedlick, "should see their entryways the same way they see a picture, as something that needs an interesting frame to enhance it."

screening is *held in place with flexible, ridged rubber or vinyl splines. If they're brittle or stiff, the screening will loosen. Replace splines as a matter of course when you install new screens.*

Top-quality screen doors are made of redwood, mahogany, pine, oak, poplar, ash or Douglas Fir. Many are built with mortise-and-tenon joints, and face doweled for extra strength.

But when choosing a new door, the screen itself deserves as much attention as the style of the frame. Steel screen corrodes easily, especially in salt air; fiberglass screening (the stuff that comes in most new window screens and doors) is the cheapest solution and is impervious to almost anything. It's also matte black and fairly ugly. If you're willing to pay 8 to 10 times more, copper, bronze, brass or stainless steel screening are excellent, corrosion-resistant options. (Nickel, monel or titanium screens are also available, if price is really no object.) Copper is the softest and will, like brass and bronze, acquire a verdigris patina in time. Stainless is the strongest and

most costly, and it stays shiny indefinitely. Bronze, the least expensive of the group, shines like gold when new. All have a metallic "flash," which keeps people from running into them accidentally, and they look good. The typical mesh size for insect screening is 18 x 14 (18 holes per horizontal inch by 14 holes vertically) with .009 or .011 gauge wire. If a screen must resist bumps from dogs or kids, you can order square mesh (e.g. 14 x 14 or 16 x 16) with thicker wire (and a bigger mesh size) for better durability. Don't put copper, bronze or brass on aluminum doors, however, because galvanic corrosion will eat at the door.

When replacing a screen, you'll need a two-wheeled gizmo (left) from the hardware store: a screen installation tool. The edge of one wheel is tapered to push screen into a slot around the frame, the other is grooved—perfect for pushing in splines to lock screen in.

Screen doors come in a
wide variety of styles.
Choose one that embodies
the style of your house, but
don't be afraid to add a
little whimsey to a house
with a plain facade.

[**fixingwetbasements**]

AMONG HOME OWNERS, FEW THINGS CAN MATCH THE AGGRAVATION caused by a wet basement. And there's no comfort in company: According to one estimate, 60 percent of all houses in the nation have foundation leaks, and the number climbs to 90 percent for houses built with cinderblocks. Water is a home's greatest enemy. Accumulating in the basement even in tiny amounts, it can warp floorboards (even in rooms above), rust the life out of appliances and turn finished rooms into mildewy caves unfit for habitation. Just as bad is the considerable cost of trying to find the leaks and fix them.

to drain all *the water that might leak into a house, a perimeter drain must be laid next to the footings, below the level of the basement floor.*

Water seepage is like cancer, says Tom Maiorano, president of U.S. Basement Waterproofing in Pleasantville, New York, a business he runs with his sons Dean and Ron. "It shows up in one little spot, and before you know it, you've got a big problem."

Even crawl spaces and poured slab foundations are susceptible to water damage. If drained improperly, they can trap moisture and leak. Hidden from view, the problem is easy to ignore until it's too late. John Annunziata, a licensed home inspector in Westchester County, near New York City, slid around one wet crawl space and found that the beams were so bad "you could squeeze them like a sponge."

As frustrating as basement and crawl-space leaks are, many can be fixed with minor effort. "In a lot of cases, the problems occur because the site isn't right," says Norm Abram. This condition can be corrected, he says, "by helping the natural drainage away from the foundation." To do this, Tom Silva suggests clearing away plantings and gently building up the soil to slope away from the foundation, with a grade of at least one inch per four feet. (To protect against rot and insects, however, the soil should be kept at least eight inches away from wood siding.)

Downspouts can also be a source of trouble. Some end right at the foundation, where, during rainstorms, pools of runoff water can seep through cracks in the walls. Simply re-routing the water by extending the downspout a few feet away from the house can help. For bigger problems, the downspouts

A foundation coating makes the walls damp-proof—they'll resist the penetration of moisture—but not waterproof. The 60-mil-thick fibered cement coating is smeared on walls exposed by the excavation. For extra protection, a 22-mil-thick plastic rubberized sheet is smoothed over the cement. It forms a solid barrier that will stop water from penetrating unseen cracks.

[**fixingwetbasements**]

to find a
*reputable waterproofing
contractor, ask
building inspectors,
real estate agents,
or home inspectors.
Get the names of
some former clients.
Call them.*

can be connected to a pipe buried at least 18 inches deep that relies on gravity to drain water farther away from the foundation.

But not every problem has such an easy fix. At certain times of the year, the rising water table can force itself into basements through a phenomenon known as hydrostatic pressure, which nothing can stop. "I've seen it actually squirting up through basement floors and into the air," Tom says. In these cases, no amount of patching, regrading or drainage pipe will help. "You've got to find where the water's coming from and get it out of there."

During a particularly fierce Nor'easter in October 1996, Betty McMoran found the basement of her Connecticut home filling with water for the first time since the house was built in 1956. It was hardly a deluge: A carpet-cleaning company sucked up just five gallons of water. Still, she says, "when I saw that water, I knew it was only going to get worse." During an inspection, Tom Maiorano found the problem: McMoran's house had been built into a rocky hillside, and runoff water drained directly against the front foundation wall. To complicate things, a puddle of water near the front door turned out to be a spring, which kept the ground saturated year-round. "The miracle is that this was her first leak," he says.

When regrading is not the answer, Maiorano suggests building either an interior or an exterior perimeter drain to stop leakage. McMoran chose the exterior system, because she didn't want to rip up the carpet and floors in her finished basement. "I wanted the mess

outside," she says. First, work crews excavated around the front of the house down to the footings. They laid a drainage pipe in gravel to draw water away to a deep runoff trench dug to one side of the yard. As a precaution, the foundation walls were waterproofed not just with a 60-mil coating of tar, but with a 22-mil rubberized sheet and an inch of foam insulation as well. "It's a lot of material," Maiorano says, "but there's no other way to make sure it works." Finished in three days, the new drains and the waterproofing were costly, but the expense seemed worth it when the next storm arrived. "Guess what—no water!" she says with delight. "I ran down about eight times to check."

McMoran may now be free of water worries, but her friend Pinky Markey didn't get off so easily. After the Nor'easter, her insurance company declared her basement disaster "an act of God" and covered all damage. But to prevent another flood, the Markeys must build an exterior perimeter drain around their entire house.

Markey lately finds herself yearning for a basement-free life. "I want to do the Henry David Thoreau thing," she says. "Give me some woods, and give me a cabin. We humans can survive in the simplest of environments, as long as it's warm." And dry.

Drainage Details: 1. Waterproofing expert Dean Maiorano maneuvers an excavator across the front of a house and digs down to the footings. **2.** After the foundation is sealed, corrugated drain pipe is laid in the trench, with gravel spread on top. Sheets of rigid insulation protect the waterproofing. **3.** After backfill reaches the halfway point, a second drainpipe is added to collect runoff from downspouts. **4.** Both pipes lead to buried collection pipes.

[fixing wet basements]

With the aid of a hydraulic jackhammer, a channel was chiseled into the basement slab, parallel to one of the foundation walls.

* * *

STOPPING LEAKS FROM THE INSIDE

DURING A RAINSTORM AT THEIR NEW house in Brewster, New York, David Angley and his family found their downstairs recreation room filling with water. "There was nothing we could do but stack up the furniture, roll up the carpets and start pumping it out," he says. The cause? An inspector later found that the exterior footing drains had been damaged during construction.

They could be replaced, but a cheaper solution lay indoors: running a drainpipe along the basement wall. For $4,000, a crew jackhammered a trench into the basement floor, then dug it out so 4-inch corrugated piping with slits on all sides would lie below the concrete slab. Interior drainage systems require a gravity feed or a sump pump, which is installed in a shallow well. Once the pipe was placed in the trench and covered with gravel, a plastic vapor barrier was laid on top and then the excavation was patched with cement. "We've had lots of rain since," Angley says, "but it's been dry as a bone."

Silva's quick fix

BASEMENT LEAKS COME IN AS MANY VARIETIES AS HOME OWNERS THEMSELVES. BUT FOR THE ONES YOU CAN ACTUALLY SEE—WATER LITERALLY DRIPPING IN THROUGH A CRACK IN THE FOUNDATION WALL—TOM SILVA RECOMMENDS A TEMPORARY FIX THAT WILL KEEP WATER AT BAY UNTIL YOU CAN LOCATE AND RESOLVE THE SOURCE OF THE LEAK: PATCH THE CRACK WITH HYDRAULIC CEMENT, A PRODUCT THAT EXPANDS RATHER THAN SHRINKS AS IT HARDENS. THE FIRST STEP IS TO CHISEL OUT THE CRACK TO A DEPTH OF ABOUT A QUARTER INCH. "YOU HAVE TO HAVE A PLACE ON EACH SIDE FOR THE CEMENT TO BOND TO," TOM SAYS. HYDRAULIC CEMENTS COME IN TWO TYPES: THOSE THAT SET IN FIVE MINUTES AND THOSE THAT TAKE 15 MINUTES. USE THE FASTER-SETTING CEMENT. WORKING QUICKLY, PUSH THE CEMENT IN WITH A SMALL TROWEL, THEN SMOOTH IT OUT. "I'VE STOPPED WATER RUNNING IN THROUGH A CRACK IN A MATTER OF MINUTES," HE SAYS. THE KEY IS IN THE PREPARATORY CHISELING. "IF YOU DON'T DO THAT, YOU'LL BE WASTING YOUR MONEY."

Cutting through a basement slab is messy work, but sometimes it's the best way to banish basement water problems. The resulting trench is stuffed with a drainpipe and gravel, then sealed with cement.

[draining the rain]

DOMINICK RATTACASA STABS THE GROUND WITH A ROUND-POINT shovel, puts his boot on it and steps up with all of his 190 pounds. The shovel barely breaks the surface, its blade no match for the dense, glacial soil prevalent in northeastern New Jersey. Besides being tough to dig in, dirt like this doesn't soak up much water. Instead of percolating into the ground, rainwater obeys gravity and heads downhill, in this case straight for the house.

regular maintenance keeps a drainage system working properly. Surface drains should be cleared frequently to remove sticks, lawn clippings and other flow chokers.

When it gets there, says Rattacasa, an excavation and landscape contractor based in nearby Hackensack, the basement turns into a reflecting pool. In heavy downpours, so much water speeds down the slope that little waves slap against the house, leaving muddy marks on the pale yellow stucco and turning the yard into a swamp. "There is constant ponding on the lawn," he says. "Hardly anything grows at all." That's not how a yard should behave.

A lawn that squishes underfoot "spells doom for plants," says Jud Griggs, president of the Associated Landscape Contractors of America. "When roots get saturated, they lose oxygen, and plants suffocate." Signs of trouble include stunted growth and wilted or black-edged foliage, he says. Saturated ground also breeds unsightly molds and fungi and, where water collects in shallow pools, mosquitoes.

Yet despite the damage poor drainage can do, fixing it doesn't rank high among home owners' landscaping priorities. "Humans are incredibly adaptable," says Tom Dunbar, president of the American Society of

Landscape Architects. "A lot of people just ignore the water. They simply give up that part of their yard." Maybe the old phrase that describes the gradual disappearance of familiar objects, "becoming a part of the landscape," has its roots in just such drainage woes. In any case, contractors say that clients are often reluctant to sink money into something they can't see. They may also be unwilling to spend substantial sums on work that appears to be so simple: After all, they reason, how hard could it be to dig a few holes? But without better drainage, there will be little to admire in this backyard, which has kept Rattacasa busy off and on for the past two years. And without a professional to size up the problems and solve them correctly, a drainage "solution" could become much worse than the original problem.

To change the course of all that water, Rattacasa has brought in a small squadron of earthmovers—an excavator, backhoe, bulldozer, skid loader and dump truck—along with 160 yards of gravel, hundreds of feet of 4-inch perforated pipe and a

The bubble in the level signals part of the problem: a slope that
sends storm runoff and snowmelt toward the house, where
it not only floods flatter ground but also pours into the basement.

[drainingtherain]

like a leak

in a roof, drainage problems in a yard can appear or disappear unpredictably. Before digging up the landscape, try to associate problems with a particular weather pattern.

blueprint of the new drainage system. The blueprint was developed by Charles J. Stick, a landscape architect based in Charlottesville, Virginia, who had already designed the park-like front yard of the house, dotting it with trees and shrubs indigenous to the region. His plan for the backyard includes patios, pathways, planting beds and dozens of trees, none of which can go in until the ground gets a lot drier.

Stick's drainage system consists of subsurface water movers, called French drains; some cut across the top, middle and base of the slope while others wrap around those future patios and beds and an in-ground swimming pool. Each drain begins as a 3-foot-deep trench that gets lined with fiberglass landscaping fabric to keep out silt that could ultimately clog the drainpipe. After dumping in about 4 inches of gravel, Rattacasa's crew lays in the 10-foot perforated-pipe sections, glues them together and covers

them with more gravel. On top of all that goes a 6-inch layer of topsoil, a drainage-friendly replacement for the hard-as-a-rock dirt that came from the trenches.

To collect as much surface water as possible, the 150-foot-long uppermost trench is completely gravel-filled and has no soil or sod on top. "Because there is so little percolation," says Stick, "an open trench like this is the most effective way to intercept water from the neighbors' yards." Eventually, English ivy and a hedge will grow to cover and hide the gravel.

Each run of perforated pipe ends at a solid 6-inch collection pipe that goes all the way down to a creek in the lowest corner of the front yard. Water that gets by this gauntlet of

A Network of Drains: The landscape architect's drainage plan battles water across four lines of defense, using French drains and surface drains. Each sends captured rainwater to a main pipeline that discharges it below the house. The system depends on gravity, not pumps, to work; thus the very slope that created part of the drainage problem is instrumental in the solution. Not all sites offer such topographically helpful slopes, however. If a down-slope lowpoint below the house can't be found to drain water, drywells or other types of drains might be required. The drainage system will have to keep up with future site improvements, too. In this case, more drains will go in later on, when a stone patio and a couple of planting beds are installed near the house.

surface drains

french drains

A trench planned for 3-ft. in depth was dug down to 9 feet when a soil test showed conditions to be worse than originally thought. Here, a crewman smooths the base to ready it for the layer of gravel on which the drainpipe will lie.

[draining**the**rain]

drains will be caught in a swale, a shallow channel that Rattacasa's backhoe carved between the house and the base of the slope. The swale has plumbing too: a string of three surface drains linked by 4-inch solid pipe buried just 6 inches underground.

The swale will also fix a common yard defect: poor grading, a condition usually created when a site is first cleared. "Regardless of whether a house is brand-new or 100 years old, the yard is usually a result of how the

which measures the soil's ability to absorb water. He hits an underground stream about 6 feet down, so he takes the trench deeper to get under the water. "We're trying to get the water before it gets to the house," he says. This land is wetter than most. "The builder hit so much water when he dug the foundation that he had to bring in 3,000 yards of dirt to raise the house." Low in organic matter, some of the fill was spread across the yard and compacted by machinery. To make the ground more porous, Stick has prescribed annual treatments with an

« Contractors say that clients are often reluctant to sink money into something they can't see. But without better drainage, there will be little to admire in this back yard. **»**

builders left it," says Dunbar. Builders and owners alike put off or altogether avoid hiring a landscaper to shape the ground. But most problems can be corrected by regrading to create the right amount of slope, adding dirt to fill sinkholes or cutting a swale to reroute runoff. Sometimes, getting control of the flow requires reshaping the lay of the land entirely. The 10 feet of ground closest to the house should slope at least 6 inches downward, says Griggs, to keep water from seeping into the basement or flooding foundation plantings. Lawns require less of a grade: at least 1 inch of slope for every 5 feet of turf.

Before Rattacasa breaks ground for the first trench, he digs a deep pit for a perc test,

aerator to pull out dirt plugs and replace them with pelletized gypsum and humus.

Once the drain system is installed—a job Rattacasa estimates will take four days—the real test will be the spring rains. If runoff overwhelms 600 feet of French drain, Rattacasa can add more. Leaving nothing to chance, Stick's plan includes vertical pipes—now capped just below the surface—that tie into the perforated pipe. To catch more rainwater and snowmelt, the verticals can be connected to the same kind of surface drains used in the swale. "This way, we know we'll have the drainage we need," says Stick. "It means the difference between having a garden and not having a garden."

Trench Warfare: Broad swaths of landscaping fabric line the drainage trench (1) to keep out silt. The durable material allows water to pass while serving as a barrier to dirt and other pipe-choking debris. The vertical pipe sticking out of the trench will be sawed off later just below grade and connected to a surface drain.

Pipe Line: Water that seeps through the landscaping fabric and into the gravel-filled trench will drain away through hundreds of feet of 4-in. PVC perforated pipe (2).

Rain Drainer: A surface drain (3) swallows water that collects at the base of a slope; a drainage system may incorporate several strategically-placed drains. Each one should be nestled into a hole so the grill will be flush with the final grade. A properly installed drain should withstand mower and foot traffic.

[cleaning water]

CHARLES WATERS'S WELL IS DEEP, SINKING 20 STORIES INTO THE BEDROCK of Vermont's broad, tree-filled Taconic Valley. Clear, cool, spring-like water gushes from the well, testimony to the rugged purity of the nearby Green Mountains. To Charles and his wife, Cindy, it was just another predictably perfect part of their "little piece of heaven." Then one night, the bubble burst when their plumber called, shouting, "Stop drinking the water!"

The perfect little well in the middle of the perfect little valley was apparently an imperfect distance from a neighbor's septic tank, and the water contained coliform bacteria. In effect, the family had been drinking their neighbor's sewage. They learned this as a result of a simple $15 test, required by the state because of some work a plumber was doing on their house.

About 15 percent of U.S. households pump from private wells. Most are unregulated and the water is rarely tested.

Although city water is usually tested daily, or even hourly, its safety cannot be taken for granted: Breakdowns in city water systems occur nationwide and no region of the country is unaffected. Overall, says Paul Berger, an Environmental Protection

Water filtration systems range from complex whole-house setups to this portable countertop model with a replaceable filter.

Agency microbiologist, "our drinking water is among the safest in the world, but problems do occur." The best way to be certain your drinking water is pure is to install a private purification system. That's what Norm Abram did. He chose a reverse-osmosis system that, combined with filtration, produces safe drinking water every time he turns on the tap. But as he discovered, safe water isn't cheap. A whole-house reverse-osmosis system can cost thousands of dollars, and a simple under-the-kitchen-sink unit feeding one tap can cost up to $900 installed. Still, filtration can seem inexpensive compared with buying bottled water. Although reverse osmosis is probably the best overall choice for protecting a home water supply from unknown contaminants of any kind, there are a bewildering number of purifiers on the market. The only way to find out if you need one is to have your water tested by an EPA-certified laboratory.

In wells, nitrates are, after bacteria, the most common contaminants. They can be naturally occurring in the surrounding soil or they may be the by-product of animal waste

Along with the reverse osmosis system under his kitchen sink, Norm installed a whole-house "point of entry" filtration system in his basement to neutralize acidic conditions and soften the water. Each month he pours a 50-pound bag of table salt into the softener tank

[cleaningwater]

a water test
is the only way to know if your water is safe. Water that looks and tastes fine can still be contaminated.

or fertilizer. Radon (which can cause stomach cancer, intestinal tumors or leukemia) and lead are also common in wells. Lead can occur naturally in well water or enter the supply through lead pipes or copper pipes soldered with lead. The metal can cause severe neurological damage in young children. To treat these and other specific problems, purifiers use four basic strategies: disinfectants, filtration, distillation and radiation.

The most common disinfectant is chlorine. Metered into the line like the flow from a giant IV, chlorine kills most bacteria and some viruses, but may have some health risks of its own. One alternative to chlorine is ozone gas, which, when bubbled through a tank of water, has the same germicidal action as chlorine and leaves behind only harmless oxygen molecules.

Filters block impurities such as asbestos, some metals and man-made organic compounds like benzene. Distillation systems filter water by heating it to steam and condensing it back to water, leaving behind heavy metals and pathogens. Ultraviolet radiation uses ultraviolet light to deactivate the DNA of

pathogens, halting their reproduction.

Though no water-purifying system removes every contaminant, distillation and reverse osmosis come closest. A reverse osmosis filter is made of two sheets wrapped tightly around a plastic tube. One is a semipermeable membrane, perforated with holes each no larger than $\frac{1}{40,000}$ the diameter of a human hair, that screens out most contaminants. The holes are so small that they allow water molecules, and little else, to pass through. (Unfortunately, the membrane also screens out beneficial minerals such as fluoride.) Like most water purification systems, prefilters and afterfilters are also required in order to trap gases such as radon and some organic compounds. Reverse osmosis also flushes at least a gallon of water down the drain in its filter purging process for every one it sends to the spigot. All of which may be worth the peace of mind a reverse-osmosis system offers, not to mention what it will do for your coffee-making.

An ultraviolet system uses the light to subdue pathogens. Although it will kill many bacteria and viruses, it doesn't affect parasites such as cryptosporidium or giardia.

no system gets everything

CONTAMINANT	MCL*	Ion Exchange (Cation Water Softener)	Ion Exchange (Anion)	Activated Carbon Filters (Granular)	Solid Block & Precoat Absorption Filter	Reverse Osmosis	Distillation	Activated Alumina	Ozone	Disinfection (chlorine, UV light, ozone, chloramines)	Boiling	Ultraviolet (UV) Radiation
arsenic	0.05 mg/L		●			●	●	●				
asbestos	7 MFL				●	●	●					
atrazine	0.003 mg/L			●	●	●						
benzene	0.005 mg/L			●	●				●			
fluoride	4 mg/L					●	●	●				
lead	0.015 mg/L **	●			●	●	●					
mercury	0.002 mg/L		●	●	●	●	●					
nitrate (as N)	10 mg/L		●			●	●					
radium	5 pCi/L	●				●	●					
radon	300 pCi/L			●					●			
trichloroethylene	.005 mg/L			●	●		●		●			
total trihalomethanes	.1 mg/L			●	●		●		●			
bacteria and viruses						●	●			●	●	●
cryptosporidium/giardia	NA				●	●	●				●	
metallic taste		●										
objectionable taste						●	●					
objectionable odor				●								
color		●	●	●	●	●	●					
turbidity	0.5-1.0 NTU ***											

*maximum contaminant level   **EPA action level   ***performance standard

[bad bugs]

NO ONE WANTS A FIRSTHAND EDUCATION in the habits of bugs that eat houses. But knowing the enemy is crucial, both to guard against unnecessary repairs and to judge exterminators' proposals. Many insects are pests, but termites and some beetles are the ones that inflict the most damage. Even with termites, though, the degree of concern ought to match the critter. Subterranean termites, the most common type, nest in the ground. They travel through wood that touches the soil, through cracks in slab foundations or through mud shelter tubes that look like brown rope the width of a pencil.

termite or
flying ant? An ant has a thin waist, elbowed antennae and hind wings smaller than its fore wings. A termite has a broad waist, straight antennae and two pairs of same-sized wings.

Swarms, often containing thousands of termites, appear mostly on spring days in the East and during early fall in the West.

Formosan termites, on the other hand, are the killer bees of structural pests. A type of subterranean termite, the culprit looks so much like the common termite that scientists did not recognize it as a separate species until 1965, well after it was brought here on boats from Asia. Still found only in southern coastal areas and in Hawaii, Formosan termites form huge colonies that can cause significant damage in only 90 days.

Free of the need for moist soil or wood, the drywood termite is especially difficult to prevent or detect. Usually the only sign is fecal pellets piled up under damaged wood. The size of poppy seeds, pellets show six distinct ridges when examined with a magnifying lens. Swarming occurs from spring through fall, usually at night, and as few as a dozen may swarm at once. Drywood termites generally cause less damage than subterranean termites.

Dampwood termites include three families. All feed on very moist wood, although the Pacific coast type, the largest termite in the U.S., can extend its foraging into dry wood. Dampwoods give few signs of their presence and are usually detected by probing wet wood. Swarming times vary.

Unfortunately, a house inspection may also turn up signs of carpenter bees or powderpost beetles. Carpenter bees look like bumblebees. In spring, females chew tunnels in bare wood, then deposit eggs in chambers separated by walls of wood pulp. Usually only trim or siding is damaged; dark streaks of fecal material often appear under holes. Males are feisty but can't sting; females are shy but do sting. Damage and the characteristic streaking can usually be seen from the ground.

Several types of powderpost beetles can convert the inside of a stick of wood to powder and pock the exterior with tiny holes. Some species attack only hardwoods, favoring wood less than 10 years old for its starch content. Others infest both hardwoods and softwoods. The chart at right introduces some of them.

SOLDIER TERMITE:
Uses its enlarged head to close off tunnels to ants and its mandible to fight other termites.

SUBTERRANEAN TERMITE:
Wings have only two distinct veins and a few hairs.

FORMOSAN TERMITE:
Wings are hairy.

WORKER TERMITE:
Chews wood and feeds other members.

DRYWOOD TERMITE:
Wings have three or more dark veins and no hair.

DAMPWOOD TERMITE:
Typically feeds on very moist wood.

CARPENTER BEE:
Looks like a bumblebee, but the top of its abdomen is shiny, not hairy.

GOLDEN BUPRESTID BEETLE:
Gets noticed because of its metallic sheen. Afflicts dead or dying trees, and homes built with contaminated wood.

LYCTID POWDERPOST BEETLE:
Attacks only hardwoods, especially oak, ash, hickory, mahogany and walnut. Favors wood less than 10 years old.

CARPENTER ANT:
Does not eat wood, but can cause damage if colonies nest in walls.

ANOBIID POWDERPOST BEETLE:
Infests hardwoods and softwoods, usually in poorly ventilated crawl spaces.

HORNTAIL WASP:
Does not sting, but can pepper the walls of a new house with holes.

BOSTRICHID POWDERPOST BEETLE:
Favors woods seldom used for framing; infests indoor woodwork, albeit rarely.

OLD HOUSE BORER:
A destructive variety of cerambycid beetle that infests seasoned wood.

ROUND-HEADED BORER:
Larval stage of an old house borer.

LONG-HORNED BEETLE:
Adult phase of an old house borer.

[**duct**c**leaning**]

THE MOMENT JOAN AND EMANUEL SIDLER WALKED INTO THEIR HOUSE after a six-week vacation, they were greeted by an unwelcome surprise: the foul odor of dead animal. Its stench permeated every room of their home, so they suspected immediately that the critter had expired in their ductwork. Joan picked up the phone and began searching for someone to get rid of the smell.

beware of
any duct cleaner with a long list of tasks and a low price. Doing the job right can take two men eight to ten hours, says Russell Kulp.

A couple of calls and a few days later, Frank Troetti, the owner of Duct Dusters, was in her house to work up an estimate. Going from room to room, removing grilles and shining his flashlight into the openings, he saw no carcass, but he did find another problem: thick gobs of dust clinging to the sheet-metal walls of all the ducts in the house. They had not been cleaned for 60 years. "When he showed me the dust," Joan recalls, "I knew it had to be done."

The Sidlers are not the only home owners in this predicament. In 80 percent of the

houses in this country, heating and air-conditioning ducts run under the floors and inside the walls. A forced-air system consists of a branching network of supply ducts that leads from the furnace to each room, while another maze of return ducts sends air back to the furnace. As the supply ducts blow air into rooms, return ducts inhale airborne dust and lead it back to the blower. If there's sufficient moisture, the dust becomes a breeding ground for allergy-inducing molds, mites and bacteria, which feast undisturbed on incoming detritus and ride through the rest of the house, unhindered by most furnace filters.

When dust bunnies show up under the bed, vacuuming day can't be far off; it's not much different with ducts, says *This Old House* plumbing and heating contractor Richard Trethewey. "A visual inspection is about all you can do," he says. Follow the same steps good duct services use: Pull off

A single handful of debris scraped from 60-year old ducts (left) contains billions of particles, everything from dirt to mold spores to skin cells. Taking a break from removal chores, a duct-cleaning crew (right) doffs their respirators for a breath of fresh air.

[duct**c**leaning]

some supply and return registers and take a look. If a new furnace is being installed, Richard strongly recommends a duct cleaning at the same time. "The new blower will probably be more powerful than the old one," he says, "and it'll stir up a lot of dust."

Professional duct cleaners tout such benefits as cleaner indoor air, longer equipment life, lower energy costs and, often in the boldest type, better health. In 1996, in the first study of its kind in the United States, the Environmental Protection Agency analyzed the effects of duct cleaning in nine houses in North Carolina. "We found that using the right techniques improved [the heating and cooling systems'] air flow and overall efficiency," says project head Russell Kulp. "The energy savings over time could pay for the cost of cleaning." But Kulp didn't find a clear-cut improvement

Duct Hall: About 60 years of undisturbed accumulation left this duct lined with fuzzy tufts of grime and debris.

in air quality. "Cleaning had no effect on airborne particle levels," he says. "That's because the biggest source of indoor dust is the infiltration of outdoor dust." Kulp's study

the dust stops here

"FURNACE FILTERS ARE GOOD FOR FURNACES BUT NO GOOD FOR PEOPLE." THAT'S THE BEST JAMES HANLEY, A SENIOR ENVIRONMENTAL SCIENTIST AT THE RESEARCH TRIANGLE INSTITUTE, COULD SAY ABOUT THE THIN, CHEAP FILTERS USED IN MILLIONS OF FURNACES. HIS STUDIES SHOWED THE BEST ONES STOPPED ONLY 20 PERCENT OF THE DUST BLOWING THROUGH THE SYSTEM. OTHERS DID NOTHING. BY CONTRAST, TWO-STAGE ELECTROSTATIC PRECIPITATORS (COMMONLY CALLED ELECTRONIC AIR FILTERS) AND PLEATED-PAPER FILTERS TRAP MORE THAN 95 PERCENT OF AIRBORNE DUST. BOTH TYPES OF FILTER MUST BE PROFESSIONALLY INSTALLED AND MUST BE MAINTAINED REGULARLY. MEDIA FILTERS HAVE TO BE REPLACED ABOUT ONCE EACH YEAR; ELECTRONIC FILTERS SHOULD BE REMOVED AND HOSED OFF EVERY MONTH OR TWO.

DISSECTING A DUST MONSTER

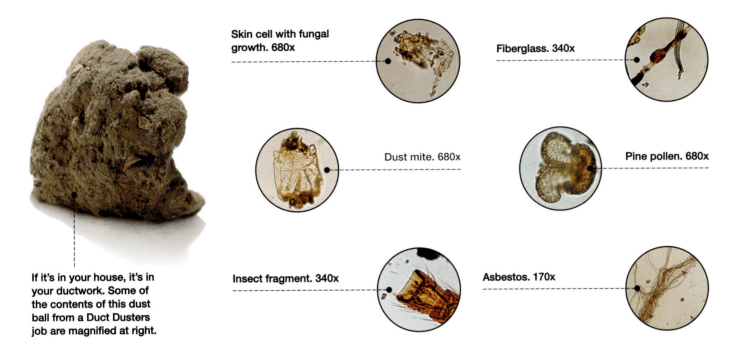

Skin cell with fungal growth. 680x

Fiberglass. 340x

Dust mite. 680x

Pine pollen. 680x

Insect fragment. 340x

Asbestos. 170x

If it's in your house, it's in your ductwork. Some of the contents of this dust ball from a Duct Dusters job are magnified at right.

showed that cleaning didn't permanently eradicate mold and bacteria— "They came right back," he says—but it did reduce their numbers. "Cleaning gets rid of the stuff that mold and bacteria grow on," says Kulp. "And less growth means that less of it gets airborne," which should help allergy sufferers.

Joan Sidler is one of them. She hadn't been breathing well in recent years and had long suspected that it had something to do with the air in her house. The Sidlers installed an electronic air cleaner in 1974; then some years ago a doctor diagnosed her as having allergic bronchitis. "I started wheezing a lot," she says, "and I felt lethargic and out of sorts. It got worse in the winter."

A few weeks after his first visit, Troetti's big red Duct Dusters truck pulled into the Sidlers' driveway. It looks much like any tradesman's pickuptruck, but it's essentially a vacuum cleaner with four wheels and an automatic transmission. Powered by the truck's 350-horsepower V-8, the vacuum inhales 16,000 cubic feet of air per minute, about eight times the volume of the most powerful furnace blower. Stick an arm in the inlet and it feels like you could lose your wedding ring. To put that power to work, Troetti's crew uncoils a 100-foot-long, 8-inch-diameter hose, connecting one end to the vacuum and dragging the other end to the basement, where they attach it to a hole cut in the system's main return duct. Then they stuff foam padding around the blower and the air-conditioner coil to protect them from the soon-to-be-dislodged debris, and block off registers in the house to concentrate the vacuum's pull.

When the vacuum starts, its turbines rev

[ductcleaning]

up to a loud whine. At full power, its nine 6-foot-tall filter bags inflate and rise from the top of the truck, its puffy columns all akimbo and swaying. "This is the only way to do it," says Troetti. The National Air Duct Cleaners Association agrees; its guidelines stipulate the use of an external vacuum source so the dust flies only one way: straight outside. And fly it does. Opening an access panel in one duct reveals an endless stream of fat gobs and fine wisps of crud. It seems that 16,000 cubic feet of air per minute would be enough, but it's not. To do a thorough job, Troetti brings out his in-the-duct assault tools: vipers and skippers.

"Joey has the viper up there for you, Wayne!" Troetti yells into his walkie-talkie. Stationed at a duct opening with its grille removed, Wayne slowly inserts the viper—a short length of rubber tubing connected to a long coil of gray plastic tubing—into the metal passage. Powered by the truck's air compressor, the rubber slaps duct walls like a whip gone wild, emitting a 250-pound-per-square-inch stream of air that blows the dust loose. The skipper—a metal ball on the end of the viper that knocks and blows dust free—is even louder, banging about like a rock in a clothes dryer. Meanwhile, other workers hand-vacuum the heaviest dust

A crewmember cuts an access hole for the ribbed vacuum hose, moved from duct to duct. At job's end, holes are sealed with sheet metal and foil tape.

deposits, typically near floor and wall registers. As the day wears on, the crew methodically feeds the viper and skipper down every foot of ductwork, cutting more access holes in the basement ducts for the truck's hose. The vacuum stops only during lunch. A short time after work resumes, someone yells up from the basement: "Hey, Frank! Found it!" A stiff squirrel lies in the narrow gap between a foundation sill and a poorly sealed return duct. A crew member gingerly transfers the remains to a plastic bag for disposal.

"You name it; I think I've seen it," says Troetti of what he's found on the job. "Marbles, cornflakes, baseball cards. Once we found a skunk nest, and another time there was a twelve-foot snake." Even new houses have problems. "If the duct openings aren't sealed, the workmen use them like garbage cans," Troetti says. "I've pulled out sawdust, plaster, two-by-fours, nails, bottles and coffee cups."

Finally, the vacuum stops for good, and the neighborhood is peaceful again. Troetti's crew is sealing all the holes they cut in the ducts, replacing all the registers, rolling up hoses and packing away tools. Joan sits at the foot of the main staircase, beaming. The smell is all but gone.

In a couple of months, the Sidlers will go ahead with a long-planned interior repainting, not only to change the color scheme but also to erase the dust stains around registers and in wall and ceiling corners. Joan's breathing woes will pretty much disappear. "When I clean the filter, the rinse water isn't black anymore, just a little dirty," she says. "I can't tell you how much better I feel."

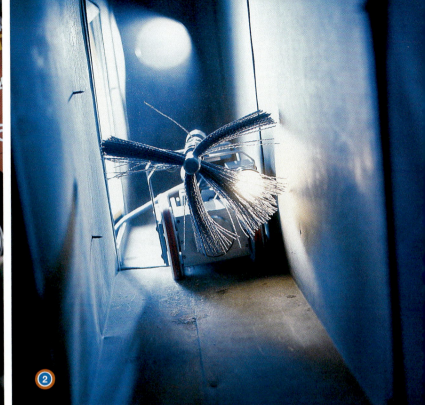

1

2

3

Super Sucker: The heavy artillery of duct cleaning, the vacuum truck (**1**) guarantees that no dust will get loose in the house. With its 350-hp engine working at a maximum 2,000 rpm, it has a suction equivalent to 130 top-of-the-line household vacuum cleaners. On one job, it nearly swallowed a customer's cat.

Duct Brusher: The spinning brush (**2**) is the fine-toothed comb of duct cleaning. It rides on a remote-controlled, air-powered tractor equipped with a tiny on-board camera. Guided by a TV monitor, Troetti can steer the rover through ducts in its relentless hunt for dust.

Snake Toil: The viper—18 inches of flexible rubber tubing—is one of several air-powered tools for beating and blowing the dust off metal ducts (**3**). Rigid ductboard, however, calls for less aggressive brushing methods that won't dislodge bits of fiberglass. Ducts with spun-fiberglass linings should never be brushed; if vacuuming can't clean them, they'll have to be replaced.

"THAT MODERN MIX WAS UNYIELDING. Once it cured, the GIVE-AND-TAKE OF BRICK AND MORTAR was replaced by A BATTLE WHICH THE OLD brick was LOSING."

[patching**f**loors]

The twelve planks lined

up in a row look like a comical **trap door,**

BUT DAVID DUPEE AND HIS CREW ARE NOT AMUSED BY THIS ALL TOO familiar patching style. Before they can refinish the floor, they'll have to rip out this eyesore and weave in a new patch indistinguishable from the old floor. Often, Dupee harvests patching strips from closets with the same flooring: New wood doesn't stain the same as the old, well-seasoned planks.

After ripping out the old patch, Dupee's son maps out a pattern that mimics the rest of the floor. On each board to be removed, he makes a few lengthwise slices with a circular saw set to the floor's thickness, levers out the old strips and makes any subfloor repairs with plywood. He makes the patch by placing the groove of a new board over the tongue of an old one, working his way across as if he were installing a new floor. To align an edge, he shims it with 15-pound builder's felt. To fit a new strip between two old ones, he slices off the groove's bottom lip with a table saw and drops the strip in, tongue first. With no exposed tongue to toenail, he drills pilot holes and face-nails with 6d finish nails. Some strips need coaxing, so Dupee sinks a 10d finish nail partway in the wood and pushes on it as he hammers it flush. When the last strip is in place, he says with a nod of satisfaction, "Now it looks original."

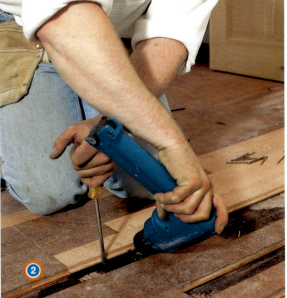

①

②

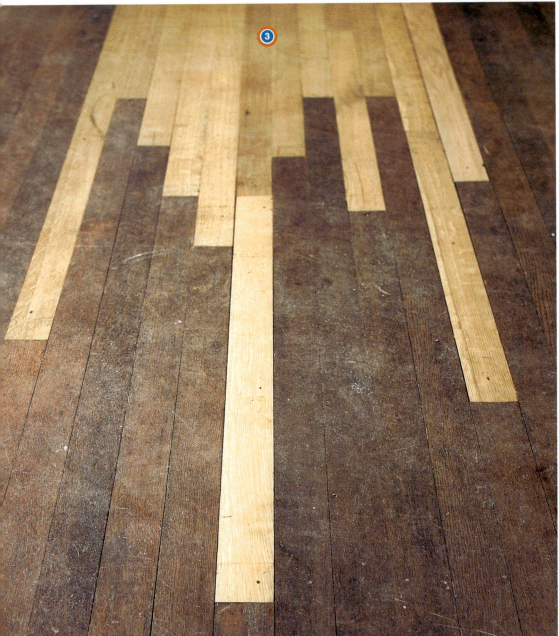

③

Removing the Old: On those boards that have to be shortened (1), Jason Dupee scores the wood with a utility knife guided by a rafter-angle square. A few chisel blows on the score make a clean, straight cut.

Installing the New: To prevent splitting, Dupee drills angled pilot holes into the tongues as he uses an old screwdriver to lever a strip tight to its neighbor (2). He then toenails the piece every 6 inches with spiral-shanked 8d nails that grip tenaciously.

The Completed Repair: When a floor is patched, the goal is a random, staggered layout (3); consistent patterns scream "Patch!" even to casual observers. To flatten any unevenness, Dupee arranges to have the first sanding done at 45-degrees to the wood grain. After that, the floor can be sanded and finished using standard methods.

[refinishing**wood**floors]

MASTER FLOOR-REFINISHER DAVID DUPEE STEPS INTO THE DINING room of a colonial-style Vermont house built in 1801 and lets out a soft sigh. Before him are 170 square feet of flooring darkened by decades-old varnish, crusty wax and ground-in dirt, not to mention a large area patched with the wrong wood. His sigh is not a sign of dismay, however; it's admiration.

a hardwood *strip floor can only tolerate about eight careful sandings before nailheads begin to show through. After that, the floor will have to be replaced.*

He's taking in the beauty of the 2¼-inch-wide red oak planks hidden beneath the abused and neglected surface.

The floors in this house were installed as part of a renovation 69 years ago. Few home owners remodeling today are likely to install such a floor. "It's a rarity to see that," Dupee says, pointing to the three-strip-wide border surrounding the hearth. "These days, most guys just put in one board, and that's it." Another rarity is the wood itself—finely grained, quartersawn, probably from a first-growth forest in the Midwest. Quartersawing is a difficult, expensive and wasteful way to slice up logs but it does produce straight, even grain and beautiful patterns. Better yet, quartersawn boards are more stable than plain-sawn—they don't cup or shrink.

Dupee has been rejuvenating tired floors like these since he was 9 years old, when he started working summers as a scraper and gofer for his father, Harold. He has never lost his affection for fine wood floors. "When we're done with a piece like this," he says,

Bathed in the afternoon light, quartersawn oak fairly glows with its four impeccable coats of clear finish.

stroking the tiger stripes in a plank, "it's going to come out and say, 'Here I am!'" He so loves this wood that he'd prefer to sand it by hand instead of by machine, which removes a lot of material and shortens the floor's life. Yet most people, he says, call him when it's too late, after the finish is long gone and dirt has filled the pores. At that point a machine offers the

Hardwood floors were once restored with muscle power—laborers down on their hands and knees, scraping and sanding. That changed in 1903 when a floor refinisher in Berkeley, California, invented the first electric drum sander; the operator rode it like a lawn tractor. The seat eventually disappeared but the drum sander remains. Now, one person can strip and sand faster than a small army of hand scrapers. But there's a risk: if left running in one spot, a drum sander can chew through a $\frac{3}{4}$-inch board in five seconds.

uneven floors,
*or floors that have
been sanded so often
they're close to
requiring replacement,
can sometimes be
renewed with an
oscillating sander.*

only realistic solution: "You can't get rid of
that much dirt without machine sanding."

So over the next four days, Dupee and
his three-man crew spend 25 hours sawing,
nailing, sanding and sealing. First, they aim a
fan out a window and tape a plastic tarp to
each doorway to safeguard the rest of the
house from sawdust. Dupee's son, Jason,
replaces the square patch of mismatched
wood (see "Patching Wood Floors", page 40).
Meanwhile, Dupee's nephew Don Fortin
searches for protruding nails, which could ruin

**Fortin swabs walnut stain over the oak, lets it soak in
for a few minutes, then towel-wipes it dry. The next day
he'll hand-sand it in preparation for finish.**

a sander's drum, and hammers them home.
Dupee notices a few shallow dips from a
previous refinishing job, perhaps 50 years ago,
where a sander spun in place for less than a
second. But he thinks the dips will probably
come out with the first sanding. If they were
deeper than 1/8 inch, he'd try to erase them with
a couple of passes with the drum sander turned
45 degrees to the grain. (If that didn't work, he

« **The cardinal rule** of floor sanding is always to keep the machine moving when it's on the floor. Otherwise, the drum will keep digging and digging. »

would replace the damaged wood.) Fortin loads the sander with 36-grit paper and uses the same technique on the patched area to make the new boards flush with those around them. After two 45-degree passes from opposite directions, a giant X of clean wood marks the patch.

Rolling the sander to the right side of the room, he begins to take the finish off the rest of the floor. A sander should always be moved from right to left because the drum tilts down slightly on the right. Making sure the drum is off the floor, he flicks the "On" switch, and the 7½-horsepower electric motor rumbles to life. Then he pushes the machine forward onto the wood, gliding the spinning drum to the floor in a shallow arc, like an airplane touching down on a runway. Moving in line with the strips, he slowly paces the length of the room as he holds back the rasping, thumping 230-pound hunk of metal pulling him forward like an angry rottweiler on a leash. When he reaches the end of each pass, he gently flares the drum up off the floor before stopping. The cardinal rule of floor sanding is always to keep the machine moving when it's in contact with the floor. Otherwise, says Dupee, the drum "keeps digging, digging, digging."

With the drum lifted, Fortin walks the machine back to where he started, moves it one board-width (2¼ inches) to his left and makes his next pass at the same measured

pace. This way, the paper on the 8-inch-wide drum grinds each strip four times. Although many refinishers crank up the drum's pressure to an aggressive 80 or 90 pounds, Fortin sets his at about 70 so that each pass gently scrapes just a little finish away. By the fourth pass over each board, the oak is perfectly clean. Even with Fortin's soft touch, sanding removes at least $1/32$ inch of wood along with the finish.

It takes nearly an hour of methodical back-and-forth sanding (and several pauses to replace clogged paper) for Fortin to scour all the finish off the 12-by-14-foot floor. The freshly exposed wood is covered with rough scratches, which he will gradually remove with successively finer-grit papers and successively lighter drum pressures. At this point, he unclamps the 36-grit sheet wrapped completely around the drum and mounts a 60-grit sanding belt over the drum and a small auxiliary wheel. Although belts are expensive, they smooth with less bumping and pulling than sheets do. Fortin follows the same right-to-left sequence with both 60 and 100 grit, but moves the sander over two boards with each pass.

A ring of dingy, dark varnish that the sander can't reach still surrounds the room. The job of eliminating this last vestige of finish falls to Ron Schneider. He gets down on his knees with an edger: a squat, heavy, wheeled disk sander that can get within a hairbreadth

[refinishing**wood**floors]

of a wall and cover places such as the hearth border, where the strips change direction. Moving the edger in short arcs from left to right, Schneider works his way counter-clockwise around the room, never letting the paper pause. He does only two sandings, first with 36 grit, then with 100 grit. Running an edger requires a strong back and a sensitive touch to keep the machine from leaving a trail of gouges and swirl marks. Edging this floor takes only an hour, partly because the dining room has no radiators (they require a special attachment). New baseboard moldings will cover the old finish in the corners, so he doesn't have to hand-scrape those areas.

Fortin isn't so lucky on the nearby stairway, which has nothing but corners, edges and narrow spaces. He removes most of the treads' finish with the edger and 36-grit paper, then sets to work with a pull scraper to get at the old finish against the riser, around the spindles and along the edge of each tread's coved bullnose. The steel scraper blade dulls quickly so he stops frequently to sharpen it with a file. Where the scraper can't reach, Fortin sands by hand. He works at smoothing the wood, repeating the same edger- and hand-sanding steps with 80-grit paper. The final pass on the tread is done with a pad sander and 100-grit paper. Scraped areas must be hand sanded. The work is slow and strenuous; the 16 treads on the stairway took five hours.

Back in the dining room, Fortin gives the floor a final smoothing with a buffer. Its powerful motor spins a 16-inch-diameter 100-

buffed once

or twice a year, then completely removed and reapplied every 3- to 5 years, wax will keep a floor looking new indefinitely.

Dupee, right, and Fortin spread the first coat of polyurethane over the stained floor, using 4-inch China-bristle brushes and working with the grain.

grit screen over the floor. In the wrong hands, the buffer can easily careen out of control and damage the surface. But with subtle pressure on the handles, Fortin has this one dancing lightly in slow overlapping sweeps. He listens for the revolving screen to grow quieter, a signal that the floor is baby-skin smooth. "We make it look like the machine wasn't even there," he says. Schneider takes the room's perimeter down to equal smoothness with 100-grit paper on a pad sander.

Dust is the enemy of a perfect finish, so Fortin vacuums each seam in the floor, using a narrow nozzle, then switches to a brush attachment to clean the baseboards, windowsills, walls and corners. He repeats this process twice to catch any airborne dust that might have settled.

* * *

FINALLY, SIX HOURS AFTER FORTIN STARTED SANDING, THE FLOOR IS ready to stain. He gets down on all fours and, with a throwaway brush, cuts in the stain around the room's perimeter. He grabs a stain-soaked Turkish towel and hand-rubs the color into each board and pore across the rest of the floor. A few minutes later, he wipes away the excess with clean towels.

The stain and the finish on all Dupee jobs are oil-based rather than water-based formulas. In his experience, waterborne finishes raise the grain and alter the wood's true color. He also believes they are less durable. "They only sit on the surface of the wood, and they wear fast," he says.

After a 24-hour wait for the stain to cure, Fortin takes glazing compound, burnt umber and raw sienna and makes a color-matched putty to fill face-nail holes in the portion of the floor that was patched. Then he lightly hand-sands the nibs raised by staining. Following three more passes with the vacuum, Dupee seals the stain with the first coat of gloss polyurethane, unthinned. "By using it straight, you're getting more of the linseed oils into the wood." As Dupee and Fortin brush, they try to position themselves across from a window, so the light reflecting off the wet surface shows any missed spots. And the men move fast; if the finish starts to set up, the brush marks won't level out. Even with the most careful brushing, bubbles always surface in polyurethane so, after another 24 hours, Fortin buffs the first coat smooth with a worn 100-grit screen. Then he vacuums three more times and wipes the floor with a towel

dampened with paint thinner. A second coat of gloss polyurethane goes on exactly like the first. On the fourth day, Dupee applies the final coat: a satin-finish polyurethane. The gloss-gloss-satin combination lends depth to the wood without leaving a overly shiny finish. By the third coat, all imperfections have been filled. The floor is as smooth as China silk.

In two or three days, the polyurethane cures hard enough to receive a protective coat of carnauba-rich wax. Fortin rubs it in with more Turkish towels, power-buffs with a bristle pad and, with a towel, hand-buffs the floor to a warm, buttery-smooth sheen. Dupee considers waxing a critical step in every refinishing job. "It has a nice luster, a nice look and a welcoming feel," he says. "And you wear the wax before you wear the poly." That makes maintenance easy.

Bathed in the afternoon light, the oak fairly glows with its four impeccable coats of clear finish. "You see how that quartersawn grain shows up more with this finish?" Dupee says proudly, his eyes fixed on the warm expanse of amber and auburn. "It's like furniture." And then, almost to himself, as a smile curls up one corner of his mouth, he says, "Yeah, this is real sharp."

[oiltankcheckup]

ASBESTOS AND RADON HAVE HAD THEIR MOMENTS AS AN ENVIRONMENTAL albatross hung around the neck of home owners. Are underground oil tanks next? The earliest fears about underground storage tanks were over leaks at gas stations: Gasoline vapors spreading under adjacent neighborhoods seeped into houses and threatened water supplies. In the 1980s, traces of industrial solvents were found in drinking-water wells in California's Silicon Valley.

Fears were exacerbated when it was reported that the contamination might explain seemingly high numbers of miscarriages and babies born with defective hearts. The worry was that once toxic fluids got into the ground, ever-expanding "plumes," like buried clouds, would contaminate wells for miles around.

Yet scientists at California's Lawrence Livermore National Laboratory and elsewhere discovered that leaking fuel oil does not always result in an environmental disaster. That's because gasoline, and especially heating oil, do not behave like most solvents. Oil can travel only where there is enough of it to saturate the soil. After that, the oil breaks up into isolated globules that bond to the soil and generally do not move. When conditions are right, bacteria in the soil will feed on the spilled fuel, converting petroleum hydro-carbons into water, carbon dioxide and other harmless materials. The bacteria are especially effective at the oxygen-rich edges of the saturated area, helping to keep the plume from expanding.

A technician for a New Jersey environmental cleanup company shovels dirt away from the fill and vent pipes of a tank being unearthed. Power equipment might break the pipes, allowing oil to spill.

The most durable underground oil tanks are protected against galvanic corrosion. Along with a protective urethane coating and dielectric bushings, this one comes with a sacrificial zinc anode that hangs from it like a white buoy.

But that doesn't mean an underground tank can be ignored. All unprotected steel tanks eventually fail due to prolonged contact with moisture. The cause is a phenomenon called galvanic corrosion, a slow, subtle process driven by the fact that steel contains molecules with differing electrical charges. As the charges seek equilibrium, electrons transported by moisture in the soil or air convert the steel to iron oxide, more commonly known as rust. Sooner or later, a hole opens in the tank.

Whether to test a tank for leaks or remain blissfully—or worriedly—ignorant of what may be happening underground is a difficult call. But know this: A leak caught early is cheaper to fix than one found later, so you might as well learn as much as possible about your system. Consult previous owners, neighbors and anything on record at town hall, such as installation or fire department permits. A house that isn't heated with oil isn't necessarily in the clear. There can always be a buried tank on the property, particularly if the house is older than the current gas line. Even new houses can be on land once occupied by older homes.

Once you locate a tank, determine its health by having your oil supplier check for moisture in the tank using a chemical paste that changes color if it comes in contact with water. Water is an early warning of rust because steel tanks can corrode from the inside out. If further testing is called for, it's best to hire a testing-only company. A company that also removes tanks and cleans up afterward has a vested interest in finding a leak.

If the tank must be removed, get an environmental specialist to do it, not a "tank yanker"—some guy with a backhoe who says, "Sure, I can probably get it out of there. No problem." And don't even consider doing the job yourself. Instead, get suggestions from whatever state agency oversees tank removal and from others who have been through the process. If the tank contains oil, the removal company should pump it dry. After adding dry ice to get rid of oxygen, workers may cut open the tank and sop up the sludge so it can't spill while the tank is being raised. Clean soil should be kept separate from any contaminated soil; the latter will have to be hauled away, while the former can simply be dumped back into the hole.

If you stick with oil heat, consider replacing the old tank with an above-ground tank. A basement is a good spot for one because it's accessible. If you must install an underground tank, however, consider a souped-up one, such as a tank armed against galvanic corrosion with a protective urethane coating, dielectric bushings at each pipe

connection and a sacrificial anode to combat galvanic corrosion. Even better are double-wall tanks. Monitors between the walls emit a signal if the inner layer springs a leak, and the outside wall can contain oil that escapes. Many installers recommend fiberglass tanks because they don't corrode, but they're more fragile and more likely to be damaged during installation (spherical fiberglass tanks are the sturdiest of the lot). In any case, make sure whoever installs the tank has pollution-liability insurance—You don't want to be stuck with the cleanup if they make a mistake.

The underground tanks most likely to leak are bare steel. Judging by its support brackets, the one below should have been in a basement, not underground.

[repointing brick]

RICK ROGERS'S TWO-STORY GEORGIAN HAS STOOD FOR MORE THAN 80 years in the prosperous suburb of Evanston, Illinois, north of Chicago. With its columned portico, brick walls and ivy-covered facade, his house is the image of prewar solidity. Up close, the walls tell quite another story.

Between the brick, slapdash patches of gray mortar clash with the original white. In some places, the brick face has begun to flake off—a sign that water is getting in, freezing and slowly turning the hard red clay into dust. A dozen 3-foot-long cracks radiate from the windows on the north side, leaving the wall open to water infiltration. Anxious to find out what has gone wrong, Rogers called Mario Machnicki, a mason who specializes in fixing brick and stone walls.

Several weeks later, Mario and his younger brother, John, arrive ready to work. "Old buildings are like people," Mario Machnicki says reassuringly as he takes out his chisels. "If you know how to listen, they will tell you why they are cracking." The message at the Rogers house is loud and clear: The mortar is killing it. Not the original mortar, a relatively soft mix of lime and sand, but a later patch job, which used masonry cement. The old lime-based mortar had been a perfect partner for the soft, porous brick, flexing to accommodate the brick's slight expansion and contraction. Like all mortars, however, it slowly eroded, and after 60 or 70 years the weathered portion was

chiseled out and replaced, a process called repointing (or pointing). Unfortunately for this wall, masonry practices underwent a tectonic shift in the 1930s. Brick became harder and more rigid, as did mortar. With the ready availability of portland cement, a hard and impervious material, masons abandoned slow-setting lime-based mortars. Instead, bricklayers adopted fast-setting masonry cement: sand and ground limestone blended together with as much as 65 percent portland cement.

That modern mix was the unyielding stuff previous masons had used on the Rogers house joints. Once it cured, the delicate give-and-take of brick and mortar was replaced by a protracted battle—which the old brick was losing. Cement dammed the joints, trapping moisture inside the brick. In winter, the waterlogged walls froze and cracked, allowing still more water to penetrate. In summer, as the brick tried to expand, its protective fire-skin literally popped off.

To repoint deteriorating brick on this house in Illinois (right), John Machnicki first must remove the high-cement mortar slapped on during a previous patching job (left). He refilled the joints with a customized mix that matched the original lime/sand formulation.

Americans' reliance on masonry cement surprised Mario Machnicki when he arrived here from Poland in 1977. In fact, before the 1870s, when portland cement became commercially available, most masonry structures— the Egyptian pyramids included— were built using only lime and sand. "It's the best mortar ever developed," says Tim Meek, a leading Scottish authority on repointing historic buildings. The key to its superiority is the lime itself. (The ground-up limestone commonly added to masonry cement is something else entirely.) This is kiln-fired limestone, slaked for up to a year until it turns into custard-smooth, brilliant white putty. Blended with sand, the putty makes a mortar that's permeable to water vapor and flexible. If hairline cracks form, rain will wash some of the surrounding lime into the gaps, repairing them. Lime mixes are easy to chisel out when the time comes to repoint although, as Meek points out, that time may be a long way off: "I've seen 600-year-old castles with their original mortar, and they're in fine shape."

For the Rogers house, Mario Machnicki had the original mortar analyzed so he could have the same recipe custom-blended. Even without the test, he learns a lot just from knowing the year a house was built. He double-checks his hunches by chiseling out a small piece of mortar and dropping it on the sidewalk. A piece containing a lot of cement makes a high-pitched ring; a chunk containing mostly lime makes a muffled thud.

The right repointing technique ensures the work will last. At the Rogers house, John

TECHNIQUES

Chip: Using a 1½-inch-wide mason's chisel and a masonry hammer (below), John Machnicki chips out the old mortar to prepare for the new. He takes care not to break the hard fire-skin surface of the bricks, which protects their relatively soft core.

Square: After cutting joints to a depth of 1 inch, he moves in with a pneumatic chisel to square the sides of the joints and blow out loose particles: "New mortar won't stick to dust."

Mix: Mortar is ready for repointing when it sticks to an upside-down trowel. To keep mortar from drying out too quickly in the joint, Machnicki first sprays the wall with water.

Machnicki chiseled out the joints, a tedious, painstaking and, for cement-covered joints, frustratingly slow process. Using an electric grinder with a diamond-tipped blade can speed the process, but grinders must be handled with skill and restraint because they're notorious for damaging brick. Mortar can't bond to paint or wood, however, so between brick and window casings he leaves a gap to be filled later with caulk. Later, when the mortar becomes thumbprint-firm, he finishes the joints.

The new patches at the Rogers house are undetectable. As always, both Machnickis are proud of that, although it once caused them some trouble. As Mario Machnicki recalls, "We sent a bill to a customer after one repointing job, and he complained, 'You haven't even done the work yet!'"

repointing rules

WHENEVER MORTAR HAS LOST 1/4 INCH OF ITS ORIGINAL DEPTH, IT'S TIME TO GET OUT THE CHISEL AND GO TO WORK.

THOROUGHLY RAKE OUT AND CLEAN JOINTS TO A DEPTH TWICE THE WIDTH OF THE JOINT.

DO NOT CHIP, CUT OR REMOVE THE BRICK'S FIRE-SKIN: THAT WILL ACCELERATE DECAY.

MAKE SURE THE BRICK IS STRONGER THAN THE MORTAR. IN GENERAL, HOUSES BUILT BEFORE 1930 HAVE SOFTER BRICK, WHICH MAKES THEM LIKELY CANDIDATES FOR OLD-STYLE LIME MORTARS. TO KNOW FOR SURE, HAVE AN ENGINEERING LAB CHECK A BRICK FOR COMPRESSIVE STRENGTH.

REPOINT ONLY WHEN TEMPERATURES REMAIN BETWEEN 40 AND 90 DEGREES FAHRENHEIT, EVEN AT NIGHT. COLD MAKES MORTAR BRITTLE, WHILE HEAT DRIES IT OUT AND PREVENTS HARDENING.

Apply: To compact the mortar uniformly, he presses in three or four thin layers with a tuck-pointing trowel, letting each set 10 minutes before adding the next.

Cut-off: Mortar that protrudes from a joint traps water. Once the mortar hardens, the excess must be sliced away with the edge of a small trowel.

Finish: Beating the joints with a stiff bristle brush makes new mortar match the roughness of old.

[cleaning chimneys]

SILHOUETTED BY THE SUN, DAVE GALUCCI CLIMBS DOWN A LADDER and away from the roof, a quiver of worn brushes and extension poles slung over his shoulder. Covered in soot, he looks like a figure from Mary Poppins. Black etches every skin crease, from his crow's-feet to his dimpled chin. Even his drooping mustache seems to have been dipped in creosote.

to reduce
creosote buildup, burn only seasoned hardwoods. Fires fueled with green wood or resinous softwoods produce copious amounts of creosote. Small, hot fires generate the least amount of smoke.

After 14 years of sweeping chimneys, Galucci attacks the black innards of a flue with an intensity born of his experience as a fireman. He knows what a chimney fire can do to a house. "I'm not here to simply clean the chimney. I am making the whole house safer."

Americans are charmed by their fireplaces. They burn logs for the rustic smell, the dancing light and the crackle and pop that warm their hearts. But burning wood produces a tarlike compound that rises up the chimney in the smoke. When smoke reaches the flue's cool walls, the tar condenses to form a black, sticky and dangerously flammable substance called creosote. It collects more rapidly on exterior chimneys than on insulated or internal stacks, and it is especially attracted to the flues found on older draft-choking woodstoves.

There are three different types of creosote. First-degree creosote is a fluffy gray dust. Second-degree is more dense and looks like blackened popcorn. Third-degree creosote is as hard as crystallized molasses and clings tenaciously to flue walls. It's the first to ignite, setting fire to the other creosote.

When creosote ignites, flames may quickly engulf the entire flue, unleashing a firestorm. Heat racing up the chimney sucks an accelerating stream of air through the damper, making the fire burn even hotter and heightening the draft until the flue growls like a 747 during takeoff. In seconds, temperatures can reach 2,300 degrees, hot enough to melt mortar, crack flue tiles and char or burn nearby studs and rafters. Sparks blown out the top of the chimney like fireballs may ignite rooftops blocks away. "Most people don't realize the explosiveness of a chimney fire until they have had one," Galucci says.

He recommends checking for creosote buildup at least once a year. Anyone who heats with wood should have the chimney cleaned after burning 1½ cords. "The best place to check a fireplace is the smoke shelf, the small ledge right above the damper," he says. "Take a knife, screwdriver or pen and scrape the wall. If you come away with a piece ¼-inch thick, it's time for a cleaning."

The only practical way to eliminate creosote is to brush it out. After closing the

How the Chimney Sweep Sweeps: Armed with his star brush (**1**), chimney sweep Dave Galucci readies for his battle with creosote. Once on the roof (**2**), he'll lower the brush and its rubber-coated weight down the chimney to tickle off the menace. For indoor cleanup, Galucci relies on a high-powered filtering vacuum (**3**); soot eats away at the magnets in a standard vacuum's motor.

[cleaning chimneys]

damper, Galucci seals the fireplace opening with a cloth tarp and inserts his vacuum's hose, his insurance that an avalanche of soot won't end up in the customer's living room. Then he heads outside, sets up ladders and climbs to the chimney with his tools. One tool is the star brush. Another, a brush the approximate size and shape of the flue, connects to a set of flexible screw-together fiberglass extension poles. Galucci pushes, pulls and twists the brush down the flue, adding 4-foot segments as he goes.

Galucci prefers to work from the roof, where he can inspect the chimney's cap, mortar and flashing. When the roof is covered with ice, snow or touchy stuff such as clay tile or slate, he can stay safely inside, huddled under his tarp, and push a brush up through the damper. When he pulls back on the brush, first a trickle, then a sudden waterfall of blackness falls into the firebox. After brushing the flue, Galucci removes the damper and reaches his gloved hand through the fireplace throat to remove any debris from the smoke shelf. If there are broken flue tiles at the bottom, it's a good indication that there has been a chimney fire, which caused the tiles to expand and shatter. (A flue relining is the only recourse.) He then scrubs the back wall of the firebox with a hard synthetic-bristle brush. In most cases, a two-man crew can do the job within 45 minutes.

Before Galucci does his dirtiest work, cleaning the firebox floor, he protects his lungs with a respirator and rubs his skin with protective creams.

Third-degree creosote may require three hours to remove with chains and drills.

For the price of one professional cleaning, a homeowner can purchase a set of brushes and poles just like Galucci uses. But cleaning may not be enough. "A lot of people think that as long as the chimney is standing, it's fine. This couldn't be further from the truth," says Ashley Eldridge, technical director of the National Chimney Sweep Guild. "A good chimney sweep is not only someone who will effectively clean the chimney but will also be able to evaluate the whole system."

In Europe, the trade is often regulated, but in most of the United States no license or certification is required. So Galucci advises homeowners to look for more than a low bid. He suggests asking for an up-to-date certificate from the Chimney Safety Institute of America, as well as calling previous customers. Finally, ask for proof that the sweep is fully insured. "You have to be extremely cautious when choosing a sweep," Galucci says. "If he does it wrong, you may only realize it when it's too late and there is a fire in your chimney."

What then? Keep some fire suppressant sticks on hand. They look like road flares but emit a cloud of smoke that suffocates flames. After tossing one into a raging woodstove or fireplace, choke off the air supply by closing all inlets and glass doors. Then call the fire department and hightail it out of the house.

Tools of the Trade: A spoked star brush (1) can be used if the chimney is close to plumb. Small brushes (2) are for scrubbing the firebox. The extension brush (3) has changed little since it was invented in 1805 to end the practice of sending boys up the flues with hand brushes.

[glued**for**good]

IN A CORNER OF HIS QUIET, slightly cluttered workshop, Norm Abram reaches for a roller-topped squeeze bottle and with a quick back-and-forth motion coats the edge of a pine board, then another and another. He cranks the three pieces together with bar clamps and the glue goes to work, its thin film becoming stronger than the wood itself in the hairsbreadth seams. Whether building new projects or repairing old ones, using the right glue—and using it right—is essential. No repair-ready household can do with just one glue.

The pale yellow glue Norm often uses is a 20th-century invention, but the simple act of gluing is thousands of years old. For aeons, the stuff that stuck was gathered, not made. "If someone dropped me off in a forest and said, 'Make glue,'" says Joe Karchesy, a forest products chemistry professor at Oregon State University, "I'd be looking at tree pitch. But it's speculation to say exactly how glues were discovered."

Inevitably, manufacturing replaced gathering. In Boston in 1808, Elijah Upton opened this country's first hide glue factory, and many more followed, becoming the proverbial destination for under-performing racehorses. Skins were rendered in a boiling lye broth, which cooled into quivering, gelatinous blocks that were air dried, then made into flakes or pellets.

Glue Tools: Using a glue roller (left), Norm spreads glue quickly and evenly. Other glue guides: **1.** Glue brushes spread hide glue heated in an electric glue pot. **2.** A rubber bulb dispenser delivers glue through interchangeable tips; a hopper-style roller spreads lots of glue in a hurry. **3.** An accordion-style injector pumps glue through a fine needle; high-pressure injectors insert glue into loose joints without the need for disassembly. **4.** An epoxy applicator (front) mixes resin and hardener as it dispenses the adhesive. A glue gun (back) melts sticks of solid glue into quick-sticking goo.

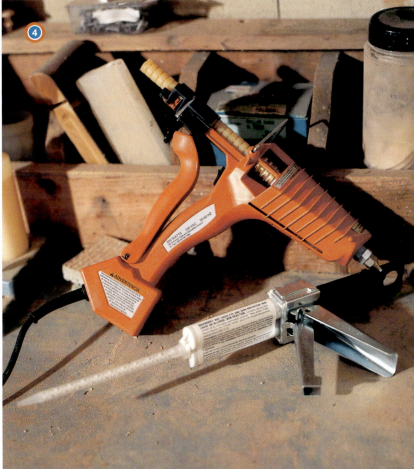

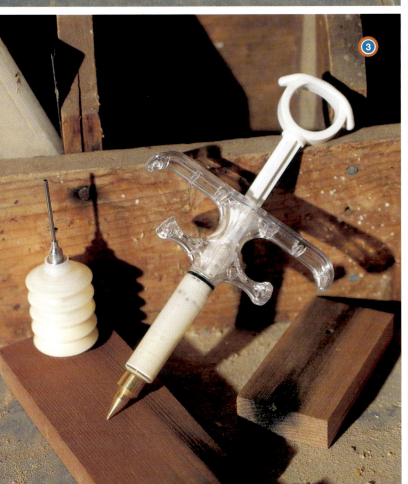

[glued**for**good]

"Hide glue hasn't changed much," says Dave Nick, an industry consultant. "It just doesn't smell as bad." Many woodworkers still heat up their electric glue pots to dissolve the flakes and pellets in water. They like the strength of hide glue and appreciate a unique feature: It quickly softens under warm water or steam, allowing joints to be reset and reclamped. Today, hide glue is surrounded on store shelves by bottle after can of sticky liquids, powders and pellets. Retailers sell just a dozen or so distinct types but under innumerable brand names. Each is good for at least one and often several tasks, but there's no universal formula that can glue it all. The only way to ensure an unbreakable bond is to know which glue does what.

After hide glue, the history of adhesives shifts from the stockyard to the laboratory. The oldest synthetics are resorcinol and urea-formaldehyde resins. Developed in the 1930s, they can bond thin veneers into plywood, bind sawdust into particleboard, and laminate lumber into beams. Next came polyvinyl acetate, known then and now as white glue. By the 1950s, most homes had a bottle of it on a workshop or kitchen shelf. Its sour but not unpleasant odor still crinkles the noses of school children as they bend over pasting projects. "I

clamp joints
just enough to make the surfaces come together, but don't overdo it. Overtightening clamps can starve the joint by squeezing out too much glue.

Glue Applicators: The arsenal of tips in Norm's glue-spreader kit include a roller and tips for injecting glue into mortises, dowel holes and biscuit slots.

grew up with white glue," says Norm, "and if the yellows hadn't come along, I'd still be using it." Strong and clear-drying, white glue is a good choice for joining wood that stays indoors. Water, and even high humidity, will defeat it.

Aliphatic resin—Norm's yellow glue—came out in the early 1950s. It has better moisture resistance and greater strength than white glue and is less runny. When dry, it is easier to sand. A later version, called type II, has even more strength and water resistance and a faster grab or setup time. "Fast grab is a big selling point for some people," says Dale Zimmerman, a technical service representative at Franklin International, one company that manufactures yellow glue, "or it can be a real headache on a more complex project if the glue gets too dry before half the joints are clamped up."

"A lot of people get to the glue-up stage and can't do it as fast as they'd like," says Norm. "It's worse if something doesn't quite fit, so test all the pieces just to make sure." He recommends choreographing the entire gluing sequence, presetting all the clamps and even numbering all the pieces. Using a polyurethane adhesive will allow more setup time.

The most recent additions to Norm's adhesive arsenal are two very different forms of polyurethane. The liquid version, the color and consistency of maple syrup, has bonding power and water resistance that exceed those of most other glues. Yet the formula also has a quirk. When liquid polyurethane cures, it foams, expanding to three or more times its initial volume and often oozing out of even a

Hot-melt glue, squeezed from an electric gun to bond wood in seconds, is handy for crafts and model making. It's also great for making quick repairs that can't easily be clamped. Cyanoacrylate, the super glue that Eastman Kodak accidentally discovered in 1958, bonds nearly as fast but is expensive for anything besides small fixes like regluing lifted veneers. Two-part epoxies are a high-strength adhesive that excels at filling gaps and holes. Contact cement is the best choice for bonding wood veneers and plastic laminates to wood, plywood and particleboard. Another characteristic of contact cement that makes it handy for repairs is its ability to bond instantly, without clamping. Simply spread a thin layer on mating surfaces, let them dry

« **There's no universal** formula that can glue it all. The only way to ensure an unbreakable bond is to know which glue does what. »

tightly clamped joint. This tendency to bubble can help fill small gaps but, says Norm, can also be a nuisance. "I have to come back and scrape off the excess." His favorite is a marine-grade polyurethane adhesive sealant, which he first used on some redwood window frames. "The stuff is so strong you'd have to destroy the pieces to get them apart," he says. "But it still has a bit of flex, and that's important. People don't realize how much wood moves."

Beyond hide glues, powder-resin mixes and whites, yellows and polyurethanes is a quartet of more specialized wood adhesives.

until no longer sticky, then press them together. The new low-solvent formulations—developed to comply with state and federal air-quality laws—contain about 90 percent fewer volatiles than their highly flammable predecessors.

Most woodworking projects, even sizable ones, consume only small amounts of glue, but it may be tempting to buy a large quantity to get a lower price. With some glues that can be a mistake because they have a limited shelf life. "Buy the smallest size you need," Norm says. "And for many glues freezing must be avoided, so don't store them in an unheated garage."

[gluedforgood]

CONTACT CEMENT

EPOXY

scrape off
old glue before regluing a joint, and don't use glue past its prime. Signs of old glue include clumping, separation and excessive viscosity.

CONTACT CEMENT: Best for bonding laminates and veneers. **Pros:** High water resistance; economical for countertops and large surface areas; water-based formulations are less hazardous than solvent-based types. **Cons:** Instant bond doesn't allow shifting after coated surfaces touch.

EPOXY: Liquid resin and hardener mix for small repairs and filling holes. **Pros:** Waterproof; great strength; flexible; can be built up outside of a joint to increase strength. **Cons:** Expensive; curing can take up to several days; noxious fumes; difficult cleanup.

HIDE GLUE: Durable classic available in liquid as well as flakes and pellets that dissolve in water. **Pros:** 30-minute open time; very strong; water solubility allows disassembly. **Cons:** Not for outdoor use; mixing requires heated glue pot; mixed batches must be discarded daily.

RESORCINOL: Resin-powder mix good for wood that often will be wet or submerged. **Pros:** Sands well; great strength. **Cons:** Deep maroon color stains wood; expensive; narrow temperature range for application; skin irritant; incompatible with unmixed resin or sanding dust.

UREA-FORMALDEHYDE: Works well on indoor and outdoor projects. **Pros:** High strength; excellent water resistance; easy to prepare. **Cons:** Portions must be measured very carefully; mixture is thin and runny; dried glue is brittle; glue off-gasses formaldehyde as it cures.

YELLOW GLUE: Original formula good for interior projects. Advanced type II formula has enough water resistance for some outdoor uses. **Pros:** Inexpensive; sands more easily than white glue; cleans up with water; very strong bond. **Cons:** May set too quickly for complicated assemblies.

WHITE GLUE: Nontoxic formula useful for assembling wood toys and other lightweight joinery. **Pros:** Inexpensive; cleans up with water; invisible glue line; can be stored for years. **Cons:** Poor water resistance; clogs sandpaper; relatively weak strength.

POLYURETHANE LIQUID: Strong moisture-curing formula for indoor and outdoor projects. **Pros:** Long open time; can be used on wood with high moisture content; foams during cure to fill gaps. **Cons:** Relatively expensive; foaming action forces glue out of joint and onto wood.

POLYURETHANE MASTIC: Marine-grade adhesive-sealant with great bonding strength; gap-filling ability. **Pros:** Super strong; waterproof; excellent for filling gaps. **Cons:** Expensive; messy application; not for use in visible areas or fine woodworking projects.

HOT MELT GLUE STICKS: Thermoplastic adhesives dispensed by electric glue gun harden within seconds. Good for simple, quick repairs. **Pros:** Easy to use; no clamping. **Cons:** At 250°F., glue can burn skin; extremely short working time; excess can't be sanded; relatively low strength.

CYANOACRYLATE: Super glues bond almost instantly; ideal for models, carving projects, small repairs. **Pros:** Clamping requires only finger pressure; fast assembly; available in gel form to fill small gaps. **Cons:** Won't adhere to porous woods; bonds skin.

HIDE GLUE

RESORCINOL

UREA-FORMALDEHYDE

YELLOW GLUE

WHITE GLUE

POLYURETHANE LIQUID

POLYURETHANE MASTIC

HOT MELT GLUE STICKS

CYANOACRYLATE

[preventing ice dams]

THERE'S NOT MUCH ROOM TO WORK ON THE NARROW PATCH OF ROOF OVER the back of Steve Thomas's house. To avoid a mishap, Steve and Tom Silva step carefully around each other, the tools in their belts sometimes colliding and jangling. Plagued one winter by ice dams that damaged walls and floors, Steve is eager to fix his roof right.

to locate
heat leaks, says Tom, examine a roof after a heavy frost to see where the ice melts first. That's where the roof could develop an ice dam.

He's also eager to pick up some tools and tackle a project, having done his share of renovating over the years. "Nice to be doing some real work," he says with obvious enjoyment as he strips off shingles with the claw of his hammer.

"That's because you don't do it every day," Tom shoots back as he removes a few feet of gutter. The morning is mild, but with rain in the forecast, there's a sense of urgency about getting the job done as soon as possible.

"Here's part of the problem," Tom says after cutting out a square of plywood sheathing. He has uncovered two recessed lights in the ceiling just below. "Talk about heat loss," he adds. Unlike the sealed can lights made today, these can't be covered with batt or loose-fill insulation. Not only are they an easy escape route for room heat, but with the bulbs just

inches from the roof, they're also a snow-melting hot spot. Tom and Steve edge past the hole to collect some sheet metal and rigid foam insulation to make airtight, fire-proof caps over the lights. That will be the first of several fixes.

Ice dams are an exasperating trick of nature and architecture. They form when warm air, escaping from a house through vent pipes, a poorly insulated attic, recessed lights or any other heat leak, melts snow on the roof (see drawing on page 71). Water trickles down the shingles only to refreeze at the cold eaves, which have no building heat beneath them. As layers of ice

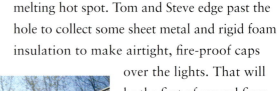

Tom Silva and Steve Thomas tackled a wintertime ice-damming problem by stripping off Steve's old roof one summer (above). Icicle spears hanging from an eave (right) are one symptom of the household heat loss that eventually causes ice dams and water leakage.

ripping off

a roof calls for care and good housekeeping skills. A loose shingle lying on a roof can turn into a skateboard when stepped on. Remove debris as you create it.

TECHNIQUES

Trouble Spots: With the plywood roof sheathing exposed, Tom cut away portions to uncover trouble spots. Steve knew that flashing around the skylight leaked heat, but opening up the roof revealed more problems. Excessive amounts of heat were also escaping through recessed light fixtures (notorious for their ability to suck heat through a ceiling), a vent pipe and inadequate insulation.

Keeping the Heat In: Where insulation was scant, Steve and Tom filled the rafter bays with cellulose. Installing cardboard baffles over cellulose or loose-fill fiberglass insulation maintains the ventilation path and prevents the insulation from drifting when air blows through. The baffles are typically stapled to the underside of the sheathing.

accumulate, they form a ridge—the dam—that blocks the flow of continued snowmelt, forcing water to pool and back up under the shingles. When conditions are right—a constant, deep blanket of snow, a string of sunny days and frigid nights—ice dams are all but inevitable. Along with the heat leaks, other contributors to the problem include clogged gutters and badly designed roofs, especially those with shallow pitches. If the backed-up water penetrates the roof's tar paper and sheathing, it can flow surreptitiously along rafters and down into wall cavities, soak and ruin plaster and even stream out of walls and ceilings.

Outside, gutters that fill with ice can bend, break and fall off. It might even seem as if gutters were as much to blame for the formation of ice dams as heat loss, but their role is more of a supporting one. "Gutters just add to the problem," Tom says, "they don't cause it, and taking them down would only cause other problems." Exposed as they are, gutters get even colder than the eaves they hang from, often causing water and snow to turn to ice that remains until the next thaw. Eventually, ice from the dam and the gutter can become one big hunk that's all but impossible to remove.

Water Shield: Installing the self-adhering waterproofing membrane was, according to Tom, "a little like tangling with a giant roll of flypaper." Two courses of this waterproof layer were laid in a 6-ft wide strip along the eaves to protect the house from water that backs up behind an ice dam.

Improving Ventilation: Tom and Steve created a screened intake at the top of the fascia board, behind the gutter. The extra ventilation will help to prevent snow from melting. New shingles protect the waterproof membrane. The rubbery membrane is self-sealing, so nailing through it wasn't a problem.

"The only way to prevent it is with heat cable in the gutter and downspouts," Tom says, "but that's really just a Band-Aid and doesn't fix the problem." Using a snow rake to keep the roof clear can forestall both damming and gutter woes, but it's not a permanent solution either, nor is it always successful. On roofs where snow has been raked from the lower part of a pitch, ice dams can form higher up. The only real fix, Tom says, is to block the heat loss and get the roof cold.

Like many old buildings, Steve's 1836 home consists of a main dwelling with numerous scabbed-on additions. The roof that suffered from the past winter's dams lies over a two-story addition from the early 1900s. "Your insulation is really thin over here," Tom says, looking down into a rafter bay with a scant three inches of loose-fill cellulose. Where Steve lives, just north of Boston, there should be at least 10 inches. To make up the difference, Steve and Tom shake more cellulose into the rafter bays; bits of it fly about, clinging to clothes and tools like dingy snowflakes. Then they level it off and leave two inches open at the top of the bay so outside air can flow in through vents and along the underside of the roof to keep it as cold as possible. With

TECHNIQUES

Plumbing Vents: An uninsulated plumbing vent introduces both heat and moisture to an attic. Tom wrapped this vent pipe with foil-faced insulation and then covered it with loose-fill cellulose. He sealed cracks at the ceiling with silicone caulk.

Skylights: A poorly installed skylight causes trouble. If air from the house reaches the underside of the skylight flashing, it can melt any snow above. The solution: seal gaps in the framing around the skylight using urethane foam sealant.

Can lights: Recessed lights in tightly sealed cases are now available, but Steve's leaked air. Tom capped them with sheet metal and rigid foam insulation sealed with silicone caulk. For fire safety, he left 3-inches of clearance between caps and lights.

plugging
heat leaks offers benefits beyond the banishment of ice dams. It also saves money by cutting heating costs.

heat leaks plugged and insulation brought up to snuff, the next step is to improve ventilation in the roof. Soffit and ridge vents are the common solution, but getting more air into Steve's roof is going to take some doing. "You've got a vent in the main part of the roof, so we need to open this pitch up to it," Tom says, pulling a pencil from his tool belt and sketching a plan on the exposed plywood. "We can notch this beam," he says, referring to a 2x12 that separates the two pitches, "but we need a way to get air into the soffit." As with many houses, there isn't enough space under the eave to add a soffit vent. "Why don't we put that plastic mesh behind the crown molding?" asks Steve, taking out his own pencil to draw an eave detail. The mesh he has in mind is a fibrous material that's normally used as a spacer to promote air circulation under wood shingles, hence the product's name: "Cedar Breather."

Tom likes the idea and draws furiously on his plywood sketch pad. A double layer of the

mesh will maintain a half-inch gap between the crown molding and the fascia, feeding air to the rafter bays through slots cut into the fascia. (Another way to create the gap is with spacer blocks nailed to the fascia and covered with insect screen. The crown molding is nailed to the blocks.) The mesh idea looks good, so Tom gives Steve a nod and they get back to work.

With preventive measures in place—caps over the lights, beefed up insulation and better venting—Steve and Tom decide to improve the roof's ability to fend off a leak in case a dam does form. "Even a well-designed roof can get a dam," Steve says. "For example, with enough snow, the roof vents can be blocked."

After replacing the sections of plywood sheathing they cut out, Tom and Steve roll out two courses of a thin, 39-inch-wide waterproof membrane along the edge of the roof and cover it with shingles. Made of polyethylene and rubberized asphalt, the membrane is the last line of defense if an ice dam forms and water gets in under the shingles. Because the material

THE DAMAGE BEGINS WHEN ICE BUILDS UP A WALL HIGH ENOUGH TO TRAP WATER, WHICH THEN BACKS UP AND SEEPS UNDER THE SHINGLES. WHEN IT LEAKS INTO A CEILING OR WALL, THE WATER CAN SOAK AND DEPRESS INSULATION, RENDERING IT ALL BUT USELESS. EXCESSIVE MOISTURE IN WALLS CAN ALSO CAUSE BLISTERING ON PAINTED SIDING. WHEN WATER SOAKS INTO PLASTER OR DRYWALL, IT CAN LEAVE STAINS OR EVEN SEND PIECES CRASHING TO THE FLOOR. AT STEVE'S HOUSE, INFILTRATING WATER WRECKED PLASTER AND LEFT INDELIBLE WHITE SPOTS ON WOOD FLOORS IN ONE OF THE BEDROOMS. AND A GUTTER THAT COLLECTS ICE, AS OFTEN HAPPENS, CAN BEND, BREAK OR EVEN BE FORCED TO LEAVE THE EAVE.

Pool of melted snow

Roof shingles

ICE DAM

Big icicles

gutter

Unvented eave

Wet, sagging insulation

what the dam does

is self-sealing, shingle nails won't be leak points, which makes the membrane better than common tar paper. It'll take one tall dam to push water six feet up the roof and defeat the membrane. Other measures, such as running heat cable to melt drainage channels into the dam or adding an apron of slippery metal roofing to prevent snow from accumulating, can minimize or eliminate ice dams. But the waterproof membrane, Steve and Tom agree, is the most reliable solution and, because it's hidden by shingles, the best looking.

If the worst happens and water enters the house, there are ways to stem the flow. Hacking drainage channels into the dam with an axe isn't recommended because it's clearly perilous up on a frozen roof, and chances are good that axe blows will cut the shingles.

Tom's quick-fix solution is to set up window fans next to gable vents or near soffit vents to blow cold outside air into the attic. This can quickly lower the temperature in the attic, make the roof colder and refreeze the snowmelt. In most cases, Tom says, the flow of water stops within minutes.

By late afternoon, the men have nailed fresh shingles in place and rehung the gutters. The job done, they gather their tools and start taking down the scaffolding. It's been a long day working on a sloped surface, and Steve is feeling it. He rubs his shoulders and makes circles with his aching arms. He squints up at the sky, where, as if on cue, clouds have moved in. Not the white puffs of summer but dark, tumultuous clouds, the kind that say winter isn't too far off.

[cleaning**muscle**]

THERE IS NO GOODNESS IN GRUNGE, THAT SERIOUS ACCUMULATION OF dirt, grime and who-knows-what that stubbornly resists attack by even the stoutest standard cleaners. Grunge laughs at grocery-store sprays. Trisodium phosphate, mixed with water, is an old stand-by that often succeeds on moderately tough jobs. But when the need to clean is urgent and your to-do list includes the grunge of a garage floor or weathered deck, it's time to call in a specialist.

store
heavy-duty cleaners out of reach of children, and where the products won't freeze.

Cleaning an old concrete garage floor—impregnated with oil, grease, gasoline gum and other products of a petroleum-based economy—is no job for a perfectionist. Short of excavating the slab and pouring a new one, the only way to restore such a floor to pristine condition is to use a high-velocity water sprayer called a pressure washer. You can rent the tool, but be careful: used improperly it can erode cement and plow furrows in wood.

As an alternative, check with mail-order companies that supply car-detailing products.

You should be able to find cleaners that do the job better than degreasers or bleach. One two-part system comprises a non-acidic solution (applied with muscle power and a wire brush) to lift grease, followed by a stain remover. Although the remover should be hosed off immediately, leaving it on for up to 5 minutes can produce a brighter floor. In any case, apply the second solution very evenly and dilute with water all at once—or risk splotches. One other precaution: Keep both solutions from splashing on any treasured possessions.

do your deck a favor

AFTER YEARS IN THE WEATHER, MOST DECKS TURN GRIMY AND GRAY. TO ERASE THOSE SIGNS OF AGE, TRY A DECK CLEANER: WORK IT IN WITH A STIFF BROOM AND THEN HOSE IT OFF. (PROTECT NEARBY PLANTS IF THE CLEANER CONTAINS BLEACH.) THE BOARDS AT LEFT WERE TAKEN FROM THE SAME DECK; ONE WAS CLEANED. KEEP WOOD BRIGHT AFTER CLEANING BY FOLLOWING FINISHING RECOMMENDATIONS FROM THE U.S. GOVERNMENT'S FOREST PRODUCTS LAB. PAINT AND VARNISH WON'T LAST ON A DECK, BUT A PENETRATING OIL (WITH MILDEWCIDE) ROLLED ON EVERY SPRING AND FALL WILL PRESERVE THE WOOD'S NATURAL LOOKS AND KEEP THE GRAY AT BAY.

"THE EXCITING DAY ISN'T THE DAY IT FREEZES. It's the day it thaws, AND YOU HAVE A HYDRANT BLOWING WATER into your basement."

[maintaining**g**utters]

WITHOUT GUTTERS, RAIN FALLING ON A HOUSE TAKES THE EASIEST route: down the side of the structure—eventually seeping into the foundation to wreak havoc. But if gutters are leaky or clogged, they can do more harm than good. Chip Newman, who has been installing gutters in the Boston area for more than 20 years, considers gapped seams, loose fasteners and corrosion the worst enemies of conventional aluminum gutters.

if a gutter *sags and can't be lifted with oversize gutter spikes, try a gutter screw—its threaded end will grab where a spike would pull out.*

He suggests close inspection of the gutter during autumn leaf-removal rituals. A hint for spotting corrosion: On a sunny day, stroll around the perimeter of your house and look up; if you see specks of sky through the bottom of the gutter, the aluminum is pitted and needs repairing. If the aluminum is so badly corroded that you can easily push a finger through, it's time to replace the gutters. "They have yet to invent a maintenance-free gutter," says Norm Abram. "When they do, I'll buy it." Don't avoid cleaning and maintaining gutters because you hate going up a ladder: Hire a gutter-cleaning service to do the work.

To clear out the gutters yourself, shovel heavy debris out of the troughs with a plastic scoop or gloved hands, then flush the gutters with a garden hose. Flushing without first removing the debris is a recipe for trouble: Water will inevitably push needles and leaves into the unreachable

recesses of the downspout. Once the gutter is empty and completely dry, patch pits in the bottom and fill gaps in seams and joints with silicone caulk. Check also for sagging gutters. Gutter spikes can work themselves loose over time; if they don't hold when you drive them back in, remove the spike and drive an oversized (8-inch) spike into the traditional 7-inch hole. Loose hangers should be affixed with stainless steel screws. Fasteners should hit a rafter, or the work will be wasted.

Although not as important as emptying gutters, cleaning their exposed sides makes sense too. To remove dirt, Newman uses $\frac{1}{3}$ cup clothes detergent and $\frac{2}{3}$ cup trisodium phosphate mixed with 1 gallon of water. For mildew, he uses $\frac{1}{3}$ cup detergent, $\frac{2}{3}$ cup trisodium phosphate and 1 quart bleach mixed with 3 quarts water. Use a spray bottle and, wearing rubber gloves, rub gently with a rag.

Heat and cold—with their accompanying expansion and contraction—can loosen a downspout (left). To make sure it doesn't part ways with the elbow, fasten the two with aluminum or stainless-steel screws, the shorter the better. Norm tackles gutter cleaning as part of fall chores (right).

[ensuring air quality]

THE NIGHTMARE BEGAN ON AN ORDINARY NOVEMBER NIGHT IN AN ordinary house in central Iowa. Jim and Kristi Gubbels were in the basement of their 1960s ranch-style house when, seemingly out of the blue, their new carbon monoxide detector went off. Both felt fine, so they simply reset the detector. After it sounded again, Jim called in a heating contractor to check.

any fume *that gets into an attached garage is likely to find its way into the house, including those from spray paint, furniture strippers and evaporating fuel.*

The contractor tested the furnace and water heater but couldn't find the source of the gas. Then, as he was packing his tools, his detector showed carbon monoxide levels above 70 parts per million in the house. Most firefighters responding to a carbon monoxide call would enter with gas masks if they detected that amount at the front door. "Jim," the contractor said, "you guys shouldn't stay in the house tonight."

All the next week, while the family camped out with Kristi's parents, Jim racked his brain trying to figure out the source of the carbon monoxide. In the weeks that followed, the local gas company visited three times but found nothing. Then a friend suggested Kristi call Tom Greiner at the Iowa State Extension Service. Greiner has a Ph.D. in engineering, and a reputation for relentless investigation of carbon monoxide problems. After half a dozen visits to the Gubbels' home, Greiner made a startling discovery: The carbon monoxide in the

house was coming from the attached garage.

Every morning in America, home owners open the garage door and start the car. On cold winter mornings, while waiting for the engine to warm, they kill a few minutes adjusting mirrors, flicking a soggy corn flake off a shirt—or go back in the house to retrieve a briefcase or a toddler. Finally, they back out and close the door, not realizing the danger. Even if the garage door is open as the car warms, the air dynamics of a house are likely to suck carbon monoxide in.

No one can afford to be blasé about carbon monoxide. A colorless, odorless gas that weighs the same as air, it is the nation's number one poison, having killed 11,547 people between 1979 and 1988, reports the federal Centers for

Every home should have one or more carbon monoxide detectors with a digital display. The one above tracks peak exposures as well as current levels. To hunt down carbon monoxide problems, gasbusters Steve Klossner and Tom Greiner (at right) employ various diagnostic tools, including theatrical smoke that reveals hidden trails of the killer gas.

[ensuringairquality]

Carbon monoxide detectors range from this breathalyzer to plug-in models with digital readouts.

Disease Control. (The runner-up poison, heroin, killed half as many.) In Minneapolis, carbon monoxide calls to the gas utility jumped so much one year that the utility hired Steve Klossner, a "house diagnostician" from Lakeland Shores. Klossner used sophisticated equipment to check 50 houses whose alarms had sounded at least twice for no apparent reason. In 34 of the 50 houses, the problem wasn't one of the usual suspects—a dirty furnace burner, a blocked flue or a gas water heater with too little draw in its exhaust vent. In three out of four cases, the source was an attached garage.

Air flow through houses is subtle, particularly in winter. When inside air is warmer than outside air, it rises and escapes (exfiltrates) through cracks around windows, attic stairs and plumbing vents. Escaping air is replaced by outside air that enters (infiltrates) through similar cracks lower down on the house. This natural air movement is called the stack effect. Add a roaring fireplace, a bathroom fan, or a clothes dryer, plus a

To prevent carbon monoxide build-up in the garage, Kristi Gubbels now lets her car roll out, closes the garage door and only then starts the car's engine. If that doesn't work? Fresh air can be brought into the furnace room (1) through a 6-inch duct draped down the basement wall. In the garage (2), round ceiling vents can be connected to ducts (3) with a variable-speed tube fan that sends poisoned garage air out through a roof vent.

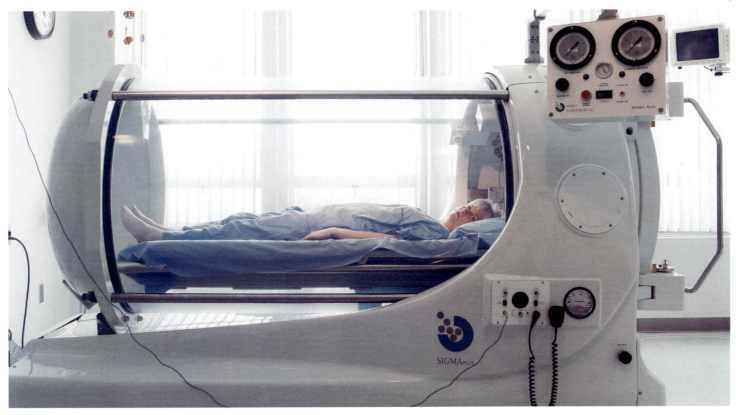

furnace that's sending hot gases up the flue, and the house needs to suck in even more outside air. Klossner found that his 50 houses drew an average of one-fourth of their outside air from the attached garage.

Carbon monoxide wreaks havoc in the body because it latches onto hemoglobin, the component in blood that carries oxygen to cells. Carbon monoxide binds to hemoglobin with 240 times more sticking power than oxygen. Soon cells can't get the oxygen they need. A headache is one classic early symptom of carbon monoxide poisoning; fatigue, nausea and dizziness are others. Higher concentrations cause increasingly serious symptoms, from disorientation to unconsciousness. Death comes within a few hours at 500 ppm, within minutes at 10,000 ppm.

It took a $5,800 modular gas analyzer to pinpoint the source of the Gubbels' problem.

One treatment for near-fatal encounters with carbon monoxide is a stay in a hyperbaric chamber (above), a high-pressure tube filled with pure oxygen. To test air movement in the Gubbels' garage (photos right), it was filled with harmless theatrical smoke. About 15 minutes later, smoke streamed under the weather-stripped door to the house, billowed down the basement stairway and seeped from an electrical outlet.

Jim started Kristi's sedan in the garage, let the motor run two minutes, then drove the car out and closed the garage door. The garage air registered 575 ppm. Air dynamics did the rest. The coldest mornings are when cars produce the most carbon monoxide, when everyone lets the car warm up the longest and when the stack effect inside the house is greatest. "Anybody who has an attached garage has the same problem," Jim says. "They just don't know it yet."

[**hvactune-up**]

"PEOPLE WOULDN'T DREAM OF driving their car thirty thousand miles without an oil change, a tune-up and a new air filter," says Richard Trethewey. "Yet that's exactly how they treat their heating and cooling systems." Indeed, like a car, heating and cooling systems burn more fuel without regular servicing. They're also more likely to break down and more likely to make everyone in the family sick.

allergies
in the family make heating/cooling system tune-ups particularly important. An investment in high-performance furnace filtering is also worthwhile.

Heat pumps and oil-fired furnaces and boilers need a yearly tune-up. Gas-fired equipment burns cleaner; it should be serviced every other year. But before Ted Weinberg begins a tune-up, he talks to the owners. Weinberg, a heating systems specialist in Eastchester, New York, asks if they're experiencing comfort problems or if any unusual smells or sounds come from the system. "Have they done any renovation work since the system was last serviced?"

Next comes an inspection to uncover leaks, soot, rust, rot, corroded electrical contacts and frayed wires. In furnace (forced-air) and boiler (hot-water) systems, the inspection should cover the eripherals—chimney, ductwork or pipes, dampers or valves, blower or pump and registers or radiators, the fuel line and the gas meter or oil tank—as well as every part of the core unit.

To complete the inspection, the system should be run through a full heating cycle. Furnaces and boilers must have plenty of combustion air and chimney draft. Otherwise, back-drafting can fill a house with toxic exhaust gas. Weinberg's crew uses smoke pencils to check the draft and a sensitive electronic analyzer to sniff the indoor air for carbon monoxide.

Next comes the dirty work: cleaning the furnace or boiler burner and heat exchanger to remove soot and other gunk that can erode efficiency. "A single millimeter of soot inside the combustion chamber can cut the efficiency of an oil boiler by six percent," Richard says. Efficiency also hinges on adjusting the flame to the right size and color, adjusting the flow of gas or changing the fuel filter in an oil-fired system.

The checkpoints for a heat pump include the compressor, fan, indoor and outdoor coils and refrigerant lines. Indoor and outdoor coils should be cleaned, and the refrigerant pressure should be checked. Low pressure indicates a leak, and to find it, says Weinberg, "a contractor should inject tinted refrigerant into the loop or go over it with an electronic detector."

If an old thermostat gets out of whack, have it recalibrated. Some thermostats have small switches, usually marked "fan" or "manual," that can be used to turn on the furnace blower even when the system isn't heating or cooling. That circulates cleaned air all year—if the right filter is in place.

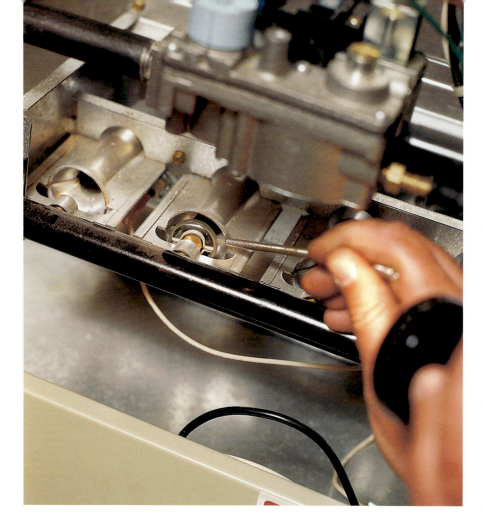

circulating pump cleaned and lubricated and air bled out of the radiators.

While thermostats rarely fail outright, they can degrade over time as mechanical parts stick or lose their calibration. Older units will send faulty signals if they've been knocked out of level or have dirty switch contacts. Recalibrating an older unit requires a room thermometer and a small wrench. Set the thermostat dial at the temperature indicated by the thermometer. Use the wrench to adjust a nut on the back of the mercury switch, just until it turns the system on. With this adjustment, your thermostat will do the right thing at any setting. Modern electronic thermostats rarely need adjusting. "They're calibrated at the factory," Weinberg says, "and they're sealed so they can't gather dust and grime."

But any thermostat, old or new, can be tricked into thinking the room is warmer or colder than it really is. The hole where the thermostat wire comes through the wall must be caulked or a cold draft will create a false call for heat. "We once found a new warm-air register installed right under a thermostat," says Weinberg. "It threw the room way off." Fixing that one required moving the unit.

Tuning up the distribution side of a forced-air system starts with the blower. The axle should be lubricated, and the blades should be cleaned. The operating amperage of the blower motor should be checked to make sure the unit isn't being overloaded, a sure sign of a dying motor or bad bearings. The fan belt should be adjusted so it deflects no more than an inch when pressed. Every accessible joint in the ductwork should be sealed with mastic or one of the new UL-approved duct tapes. "Because of its poor history, regular duct tape shouldn't be used," Richard says. Any ducts that run outside the heated space must be insulated. On a hot-water system, the expansion tank should be drained, the

HUMIDIFIER CARE AND FEEDING

An in-duct humidifier that's neglected can breed mildew and bacteria, not to mention add too much moisture to a house. A unit with a water reservoir must be drained and cleaned with white vinegar, a mix of one part chlorine bleach to eight parts water, or muriatic acid. Weinberg recommends treating the water in the reservoir regularly with chlorine or bromide tablets to keep microorganisms under control. Reservoir humidifiers also have small, slow-speed motors that need a few drops of oil once a year. Mist-type humidifiers require regular cleaning too—with the same chemicals—to remove mineral deposits. A common mistake with humidifiers is leaving them on after the heating season ends. Don't forget to pull the plug, shut the water valve and drain the unit.

MODERN MIRACLE: MEDIA FILTERS

Furnaces have a built-in dust filter that keeps the furnace and ductwork clean. Unfortunately, the type most people have in their forced-air heating system does little, if anything, to improve the air they breathe. That takes a whole new filter—one that's built in between the main return duct and the blower cabinet—called a media filter. Made of

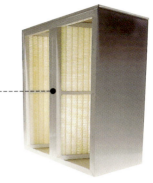

EXTENDED MEDIA. 100 square feet of cotton-polyester pleated nonwoven fabric packed into a cartridge 11 inches deep. Extremely effective. Filter lasts three years.

ELECTROSTATIC. Air flowing over plastic fibers creates a static charge, attracting dust and particles. Filtration of small particles poor. Washable.

ELECTRONIC AIR CLEANER. Charge of 110 volts attracts various particles. Removable metal filters last indefinitely. Extremely effective. Cartridges must be cleaned with a hose or in a dishwasher every three months.

DEEP-PLEATED MEDIA. Nonwoven cotton-polyester fabric consistently cleans without impeding air flow. Cartridges must be replaced every one to two years.

STANDARD. Disposable panel captures coarse particles that can clog a furnace blower. Very ineffective for indoor air filtration. Cartridge lasts 1 month.

Besides adding moisture, an in-duct humidifier can also put mildew and microorganisms into the air if its filter is not cleaned often.

[hvac**t**une-up]

turn on
*the furnace blower
even when you aren't
heating or cooling. The
longer that household
air blows through a
media filter, the cleaner
your air will get.*

a deeply pleated paperlike material, a media filter is at least seven times better than a standard filter at removing dust and other particles. John and Judy Fernberg know exactly what that means.

Nestled amid the woods and wildlife of Boston's suburbs, the Fernbergs' four-bedroom colonial made people sniffle. All the vacuuming, dusting and cleaning she could muster couldn't stop what Judy Fernberg dubbed a sneezefest. "We didn't know what we were doing wrong," she says. "It was so frustrating." Finally, after the Fernbergs' three children swapped a dozen colds in as many weeks, the family decided to call Roy Erickson, an air filtration specialist in Dedham, Massachusetts.

Erickson offered to make a diagnostic house call. When the contractor arrived, he barreled past everybody and headed down the basement stairs. From the ductwork beside the forced-air gas furnace, he plucked a thin blue panel and shook it in disgust. The Fernbergs looked confused: The filter was clean. "These 50-cent fiberglass filters only protect the furnace," Erickson explained. "They don't do people any good at all."

The Fernbergs aren't the only home owners relying on meager filters to prevent their wheezings. Most Americans who heat their houses with forced-air furnaces have the same kind of standard furnace filter. Made from loosely woven spun-glass fibers, these filters are inexpensive and readily available, but won't trap many particles smaller than 10 microns and so allow bacteria, smog, molds, asbestos fibers and tobacco smoke to pass right through. To stop the tiny toxins,

Erickson convinced the Fernbergs to upgrade to a pleated media filter that would cleanse the air of everything from insecticide dust to flu viruses. Studies by the American Lung Association show that media filters also reduce the incidence of chronic respiratory disorders, particularly asthma.

Pleated media filters are a blend of polyester and cotton folded up like a fan. Compressed, they are usually no wider than 6 inches, but the pleated material can cover up to 75 square feet when stretched out. This increased area of filtration accounts for the filters' long life, which can exceed two years. The only drawback is the filter fibers' tight weave, which may restrict the furnace's ability to blow air through the house. Filters are rated according to the blower capacity they accommodate, a crucial match that maintains comfortable conditions. "If you have too much resistance on the filter, you'll starve the fan and decrease the air delivered to your house," says H.E. Barney Burroughs, a former president of the American Society of Heating, Refrigerating and Air-Conditioning Engineers.

When Erickson returned the next day, the Fernbergs watched as he took apart the existing ductwork, attached the filter frame and assembled ducts he'd prefabricated at his shop. He finished the installation in less than an hour. Maintenance is simple, he told the Fernbergs: "Just pull out the old filter, and shove in the new one." Erickson left confident the Fernbergs would soon be breathing more easily: "All my clients have noticed a distinct difference in air quality. No sneezing, no puffy eyes, no dust in the house."

Trashing the Old: To retrofit a media filter on an existing forced-air furnace, heating contractor Roy Erickson first removes the old, 1-inch-thick standard filter (1) and drops it in the trash. Then, with a clanging of sheet metal, he rips out a strip of return duct to make room for the media filter's 7-inch-thick housing.

Filling the Hole: Next, Erickson attaches one side of the new filter's boxlike steel housing (2) to the outside of the furnace, using short, self-tapping sheet-metal screws.

Fitting the Filter: On the other side of the housing, Erickson attaches a new piece of return duct. He fits the ductwork tightly over the housing, caulks gaps with silicone sealant and slips in the new filter (3). Total installation time: 50 minutes.

[**pest**control]

ONE WINTER NIGHT, 4-YEAR-OLD Sam Tydings ran into the mouse that lived in his house. The tiny creature emerged from under a chair in the living room, ambled across the kitchen floor and squeezed under the freezer. Unfazed by the presence of humans, the mouse appeared again, moseying back to the living room as if out for an evening stroll. "Look! It's a mouse!" Sam yelled, squatting down to get a closer view. "Ooooh, you're funny. I think I'll name you Tim."

mouse or rat?

Rats often chew entrance holes 2 inches in diameter, and their droppings range from ½- to ¾-inches in length. Wipe out rats as you would mice.

Later that evening, Sam's mother was more exasperated than horrified to hear of the encounter. About a year earlier, mice had invaded the Tydings cupboard. After hiring an exterminator, the family tossed out contaminated food, disinfected the pantry and began storing edibles in hard plastic containers. Now their son was pals with a mouse.

The house mouse has followed man from the pyramids to the cul-de-sac. Unlike humans, however, a female mouse can, in a single year, have 5 to 10 litters of 7 to 9 pups each. Such reproductive prowess is disastrous for home owners. "If you have one or two mice, and you wait to take care of them, you'll have them everywhere in a matter of weeks," says Bobby Corrigan, an urban rodentologist who owns R.M.C. Pest Management Consulting in Richmond, Indiana.

We feel stigmatized when mice choose to share our abodes: My house is clean—why me? The truth is, house mice will lay siege to even the most pristine building if they can find a way in. Eliminating the threat means enacting a three-point plan: Cut off the food supply, seal mice out of the house and kill or remove any mice left inside.

Dave Walters, a technician with Cooper Pest Control in Lawrenceville, New Jersey, inspected the Tydings house not long after Sam met Tim, and Walters knows what relentless invaders mice can be. They can climb up brick, shingles or pipes and can even swim. Their ¼-inch-wide skulls can squeeze through holes as small as a dime. "If your pinkie can get in the hole," says Walters, "so can a mouse." And a mouse will widen a hole that happens to be a bit snug by chewing through wood, light plastic or wallboard. Once the animal gets inside, its scent attracts others.

Walters' inspection revealed that the builder of the Tydings house had neglected to plug openings around pipe, wire and utility-line entry points. To seal out critters, Walters shoves a wad of copper mesh into the space around the pipe or utility line, then guns in siliconized acrylic caulk. In hidden spots, he squirts pressurized foam around the mesh. "Everyone always tells you to use to steel wool," Walters says. "The trouble is, people

A History of Ingenuity: The endless quest for a better mousetrap has produced gadgets galore. **1.** Claw Trap (1876). The mouse leaps to reach the cheese on the top hook—only to be hooked itself. **2.** U-Neek Jar Trap (1909). The mouse creeps through the hole in the lid and yanks on the bait, unwittingly slamming the door. Makes ships-in-a-bottle downright passé. **3.** Buxton Impaler (1860). At the touch of a paw, the spring-driven circle of spikes crashes down upon the beastie. **4.** D. Johnson Snap Trap (1847). It could wipe out an entire family of mice in one nasty chomp, the inventor claimed. **5.** Electrocuter (1947). All that's needed is a dab of bait and a power source to make good the manufacturer's claim: "Kills hundreds of mice for a penny's worth of electricity." **6.** Bing Crosby's Trap (1940). The famous crooner's company, the Crosby Research Foundation, backed the production of these aluminum snap traps. **7.** Leg Trap (circa 1900). A blacksmith meticulously forged this elegant "bear trap for mice."

[**pest**control]

never use a grade that's coarse enough. They go with something that feels like a scouring pad. Mice can chew through that. Once they hit the copper, it stops them cold."

Holes larger than 3 inches in diameter require different treatment. Walters uses cement to seal large foundation cracks. To close up mouse entryways in garage walls, he patches the drywall with construction adhesive and squares of aluminum siding or plywood.

Where drywall meets a foundation, as in basements and garages, Walters wedges a piece of lumber into the space and seals it with construction adhesive and foam. Garages are always the toughest spots to mouse-proof because people leave their garage doors open for hours at a time. "Usually the garage attic leads right into the house," says Walters. He also makes sure that all doors to the house, including the garage door, are correctly weatherstripped (see page 116).

Once you've blocked all possible entry points, it's time to nab the beasts themselves. Of the thousands of mousetraps invented over the aeons, the classic snap trap is perhaps the cheapest and most efficient. So why do people fail so often to catch mice with them? The biggest mistake: placing traps in the middle of a room. Mice prefer to keep their backs to the wall, so traps work best when perpendicular to a wall. Another mistake, Corrigan says: "People buy a little two-pack of traps and think they're going to catch all the mice. You need a lot of traps." Place about six traps everywhere mice have been sighted or left droppings: six traps in the

kitchen, six in the garage and so on. It pays to do the job quickly and efficiently. Every day that you delay, another litter could be born.

Innately curious, mice will investigate any food source. Some experts bait with a tiny smear of peanut butter, others with a sliver of raw bacon, which forces the mouse to tug at the trigger. But go easy on the bait. Too much food and mice may nibble at it without tripping the trigger. To get mice to betray their location, Walters suggests putting down traps that are baited but not set. Wait a few days. The spots where mice have taken the bait are where you now want to move all the traps—baited and set this time. When you catch mice, remove all the traps and wait a week before trapping again. You'll stand a greater chance of nabbing those savvy mice who may have learned not to mess with a trap.

The downside of a snap trap, of course, is the carcass. If it repulses you, set the trap in an open paper bag and later toss it in the garbage—trap, mouse and all.

Poison is a quick way to get a nasty job done, but it can backfire in the long run as a population builds up resistance. Poisons are also deadly to humans and pets. The best bait stations, made of heavy, gnaw-resistant plastic, are tamper-proof—even if children and pets find the boxes, they won't be able to open them. Professionals advise against using poison pellets packaged in small cardboard boxes. Mice can tear the box and scatter the candy-colored pellets, or might gather the pellets without ingesting them. Another drawback: The poisoned rodent may die in your walls—if it doesn't stagger and croak before your eyes.

to cut off
a rodent's food supply, start by cleaning beneath the refrigerator, stove and dishwasher. Then store dry food, including pet food and birdseed, in hard plastic containers.

TEETER TOTTER: As mice enter, their weight depresses a ramp and they drop into a holding pen. Check the trap daily.

SIMPLE SNAPPER: Since 1894, the snap trap has been the top mouse-getter. The inexpensive traps are considered humane due to their quick action.

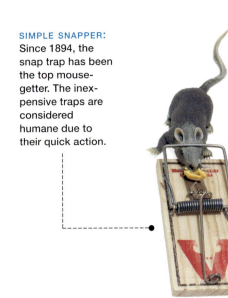

LOG ROLL: Mice trot up the stairs and across the dowel. The cylindrical baiting device spins, turning the dowel and dumping the rodent into a vat of antifreeze.

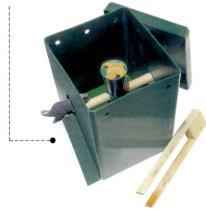

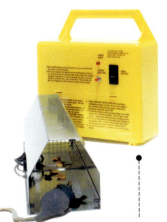

SHOCKER: Mice wander into an aluminum tent, toward a panel that zaps intruders with 6,000 volts of electricity. Very effective.

OPEN SESAME: Mice step on a trapdoor, triggering a paddle-wheel mechanism that sweeps them into the tin dungeon.

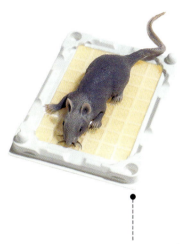

STICKY BED: Inexpensive, non-toxic and disposable, a glue trap baited with peanut butter can catch up to two mice.

SUPER SNAPPER: As a mouse nudges the lid on a food tray, a spring-loaded trap slams down with crushing force. Harder to trip than a standard snap trap, but safer for people.

TIN TERROR: Once in, mice (up to 30 of them) can't leave. Used by professionals in food processing plants.

GANGPLANK: When mice reach the bait, the over-sized diving board tips them into anti-freeze. The trap resets itself.

[looking**for**leaks]

OUR LOG-CABIN forebears would surely have loved the high-tech caulks and patching systems that protect modern houses from leaks. Yet despite the effectiveness of such remedies, water is relentless and, when it finds a path, the most damaging and wily of adversaries. There's nothing worse than the torturous drip, drip, drip from a skylight, an attic full of sodden insulation or a steadily deepening pond in the basement.

"Anticipate leaks before they happen," says San Diego custom home builder Mac McCarter, whose first job in the construction trade 25 years ago was to find and fix leaks in every one of 127 new houses in a Southern California subdivision. "The source of many leaks is not always readily apparent," he says. "When I

look for them, I feel like Sherlock Holmes in a rain suit. I've never lost respect for the amazing ways water can get into a house."

If you own a house, you'll eventually have to track down a pesky leak—No house remains leak-free forever. Though it's rarely a fun job, leak-hunting gets easier when you have the right gear. A putty knife scrapes at rust and corrosion. An awl probes for rotten wood. A utility knife cuts away decayed caulk. A flashlight illuminates crumbling mortar inside a chimney. A notepad records jobs to do and conditions to monitor, and helps create what will soon be a complete annual checklist. So does a point-and-shoot camera. Chalk or a permanent ink pen marks the suspected locations of leaks. Rubber-soled shoes prevent a slip and fall. Binoculars bring you to places all but the agile fear to tread. A caulk gun loaded with goop seals small gaps and holes.

In the battle against leaks, simple tools, vigilance and a methodical approach produce the best results. Masonry repairs, for example, often call for a small hand trowel (left), a slender pointing trowel, a cold chisel and a ball-peen hammer. Roofing repairs, on the other hand, rely on a prybar and a claw hammer (right).

[looking for leaks]

WINDOW DETAILS

At the top of a window, flashing should cover the casing and run up under siding. Check to make sure the metal is intact and shaped to shed water at the sides. At the bottom of the window, take a look at the windowsill (1). It should have a notch on the underside to stop water that—thanks to the miracle of surface tension—would otherwise flow up under the sill and slip behind the siding. Sometimes these cuts fill with paint, so check yours and make sure it's clear.

LEAKS IN THE ATTIC

An annual tour beneath the roof may reveal pinpoints of light or an open seam where water is certain to enter. Examine rafters for telltale stains. A leak can take a surprisingly circuitous route. Look closely where brick and mortar meet rafters; stains and crumbling mortar can mean a chimney's flashing isn't doing the job. Usually made of copper, aluminum or galvanized steel, flashing surrounds big and little roof protrusions, including chimneys, dormers, skylights and vent pipes. It is vulnerable to sudden temperature swings, water torrents and acid rain; over time, even corrosion-resistant metals can succumb. Inspect what you can see: look for rust, pinholes, looseness, lifting. Reseal nail heads and small gaps with roofing cement; renail if necessary. The flashing between the chimney and roof, as well as the overlapping counterflashing, must be snug and flat.

Plot a leak-point's distance from major roof features such as the ridge and vent

pipes; otherwise it can be difficult to locate the problem from atop the roof.

FOUNDATION FIXES

Water that pools at foundations can seep through and dampen or even flood basements. For surface water to exit promptly, the ground should slope away from the house at least one inch in every four feet. Spot regrading (2) can work in small areas; larger areas might call for underground drain pipes (see page 20).

CHIMNEY AND MASONRY LEAKS

When water gets through masonry walls, it's not usually the fault of the masonry itself. Instead, it's typically due to mortar that has deteriorated. Use a cold chisel to clear the way for new mortar, which is easy to mix and relatively straightforward to apply (see page 52). Water that finds its way down a chimney flue can react with acidic creosote to weaken mortar. Block the rain with a chimney cap.

Inspect the seam between the clay flue liner and the chimney and reseal with mortar or caulk as needed.

QUICK ROOF REPAIRS

Small roof leaks can be sealed with roofing cement, but a missing, lifted, curled or cracked shingle should be replaced. Remove old nails with a flat pry bar and pull out the bad shingle. Seal holes with roofing cement. Work a new shingle back in place under the overlapping shingles, fasten it with galvanized roofing nails and seal the heads with cement. Shingles in tricky spots, such as along ridges and hips and against flashing, should be repaired, not replaced. If they're totally shot, hire an expert. If wood shingles must be replaced, soak replacements in water for a few hours: that mimics the swelling after a rain and lessens the chance of nail pop.

On Leak Patrol: 1. Some window leaks announce themselves with drips and water stains, but others stay hidden. The cause may be subtle, such as a clogged dripstop. 2. Water ought to flow away from a house, not towards it. Check every spring for wrong-sloping areas and regrade them. 3. If one mortar joint leaks, check carefully for others; the problem may be widespread. 4. To seal asphalt pavement, pressure-wash the surface, let it dry, and apply sealer with an extra-large roller or a short-bristle broom.

[replacing a threshold]

For many centuries, a threshold

has been the symbol of welcome.

But a threshold is also a weak point in the protective envelope of a home. It is here that water and cold air can make their way into even the sturdiest structure. Tom Silva cautions that a less-than-perfect threshold, like the one he replaced on a door in Reading, Massachusetts, is an open invitation to water.

"Cracks, rot, broken pieces—any signs of water infiltrating—you don't want that to go for too long," Tom says.

Although the Reading house's back door threshold was relatively new (it had been in place only 12 years), one edge was already broken, a victim of weather and wear. Rather than patch the damage and hope that it would hold together, a tall order in such a high-traffic, exposed location, Tom opted to replace the threshold with a sturdy new one cut from oak. He also took the opportunity to waterproof the sill beneath to stave off future damage. "Rot grows fast. If you don't stop it right away, you end up with a sill problem rather than a threshold problem, and then you're

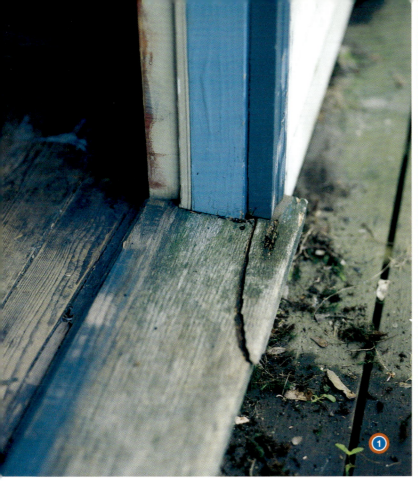

The Damage: The exposed "horns" of an exterior door's threshold (1) are particularly vulnerable to damage. Weakened by weather and stepped on incessantly, the wood will eventually give way if not cared for properly.

Out With the Old: To remove the old threshold, Tom slices it deftly in half (2) with a reciprocating saw (as here) or a handsaw, being careful not to damage the sill beneath. Then he pries the wood out with his hammer.

Making a Template: Tom uses the pieces he has removed as a template for marking the notch at both ends of the new threshold (3). He separates them a pinch to make up for what the sawblade ate and measures to be sure he matches the true length. Then he cuts the new stock along his marked lines.

Waterproofing the Sill: While the sill is exposed (4), Tom water-proofs it with a layer of self-adhesive rubberized membrane, which acts as flexible flashing. Water that splashes in front of the threshold won't be able get past the flashing to work its wood-rotting mischief on the sill. "This is just a little added insurance," he says.

On to the Threshold: Tom coaxes the thickest part of the threshold past the jamb with a little help from his hammer and a scrap block of wood (5), then shims the entire board up to fit flush against the jamb. Silicone sealant, construction adhesive and expanding-foam insulation slipped into crevices beneath the threshold are the best materials to hold it in place; nails driven through the top would simply invite cracks and water seepage.

Now for the Door: Once the threshold is in place, Tom checks the fit of the door and makes sure its weatherstripping is intact. In this case, he had to remove a bit from the door bottom to get a good fit with the threshold. Slipping new weatherstripping (6) into a router-cut channel completed the job.

really looking to spend some money," he says. Replacing a sill is structural work that nobody ever looks forward to; replacing a threshold, however, is not too difficult. It's a job best tackled when the weather is still warm enough to leave the door open for a couple of hours.

Though it's tempting to root out a problem threshold right away, Tom started deliberately, as he always does, by making some measurements. First he determined the overall length of the old threshold by measuring between the "horns," the two stubs that project under the door casing on the outside of the house, and cut the oak threshold stock to length. Then he made a pencil mark about midway along the old threshold, and measured from one side of the doorway in to the pencil line, transferred this dimension to the new threshold and repeated the step to get a measurement from the other side. These location marks will help him position the new threshold later on.

After using the pieces of the old threshold as a template to mark out the shape of the new one, Tom made partial cuts along his layout lines with a circular saw, then switched to old-fashioned manpower and a handsaw to complete the notches precisely.

Coaxing the threshold into place, Tom secured it to the sill and turned his attention to the other side of the threshold equation: the door. The bottom of the door shouldn't bind against the new sill, but it also can't swing so freely that cold air floods over the threshold and into the house. After taking the door off its hinges, Tom trimmed it down using a power plane and routed a $\frac{1}{8}$-inch-wide, $\frac{3}{8}$-inch-deep groove in the bottom edge for a spline of nylon-pile weather stripping. After brushing the newly exposed wood with water-repellent primer, Tom stepped back to regard his work. Now for the first step.

Once the threshold is secure, Tom troubleshoots the fit of the door and its weather stripping. If necessary, he'll use a power plane to trim a bit from the end of the door before adding new weather stripping.

[**stair**repair]

AS TOM SILVA POINTS OUT, THERE there are many things besides careening furniture and rough-housing kids that can break a stair baluster: "An ax, a baseball bat, a saw…" He's only half-joking: The stair of every old house gets battered and abused in ways its builders never anticipated, and the slender spindles end up with more than their share. Loose or broken balusters might not jeopardize the balustrade, but making timely repairs could keep kids from tumbling off the staircase.

balusters
can be loosened by a poorly secured handrail. Check the handrail's connections at each end and tighten them if necessary.

It's possible to repair a broken baluster without removing it, but a patch, though it might look perfect, will always be weak. And as Tom will tell you, doing the job right is always better in the long run, particularly when safety is involved.

The first step is to extract the damaged spindle, or an adjacent one if the spindle is missing entirely (you'll need an example when you shop for a replacement). At the bottom end of every baluster is tenon—a stub of wood—that fits into a hole, called a mortise, that's notched into the tread. Sometimes the tenon is cylindrical, but older stairs often have dovetailed tenons whose angular surfaces prevent a baluster from twisting. What you'll find at the other end of a baluster depends on its silhouette. Balusters with squared tops, such as the ones in this project, are often just cut off at an angle and toenailed into the underside of the handrail. Gracefully tapered balusters, on the other hand, often fit into a hole in the stair's handrail.

To remove a baluster, start by prying off the return, a small piece of wood that covers up the end of the tread. A dovetailed tenon will slip right out. Then wiggle the top of the baluster free or, if it's nailed, coax it with a hammer. David Raymond, a carpenter in Fairfield, Connecticut, rests a small block of scrap wood against the top of the spindle and strikes the block with a mallet, a technique that prevents him from leaving ugly bruises on the handrail.

Once the baluster is out, you'll have to find a mate for it. This will either be the easiest part of the whole job or the most dreadful—old stair parts can be tough to match. There are usually two or three balusters per step, each a different length, so pay attention to length as well as shape (and wood species, if the baluster will be clear-finished). Check local lumber yards first. If you can't find a match there, try the Internet; some mail order companies stock a marvelous selection of replacement balusters. If you strike out there, you must have a replacement custom-made by a woodturner (a woodworker who specializes in lathe work). In any case, says Tom, purchase an extra baluster or two and

A stair restored rekindles a
sense of elegance as well
as a feeling of safety.

TECHNIQUES

First Step: Grand results start simply. One of the balusters was missing altogether, so carpenter David Raymond had to remove its neighbor to use as a template. To free the lower end, he scored the seam between the tread return and the tread, then pried off the return (above) using the fan-shaped end of a small cat's paw. Two or three finishing nails typically hold the return in place.

Broken, missing or mismatched balusters turn an elegant balustrade into a hockey-player's grin. Fixing the problem isn't difficult; it's finding matching replacements that can be exasperating.

set them aside for future repairs. The replacements should be slightly long so you can trim them perfectly to fit the stair.

Depending on how long a turner takes to make the replacements (or how many lumber yards you visit), you'll have plenty of time to clean up the wood in and around the baluster holes-in-waiting. Scrape out globs of old finish and lightly clean off glue or dried finish from the end of the tread and the mating surface of the return, using fine sandpaper.

Trimming the new baluster to fit calls for careful measurement and the assistance of a sliding bevel gauge to replicate the angle. In old houses, balusters are often out of plumb, and Raymond says you ought to resist the temptation to install new ones plumb—they'll make the others look like crooked teeth. "Ultimately," he adds, "it's about what the eye picks up." If it looks right, it is right.

Sand and paint a baluster before you install it, as Raymond does. Later, when you've cut it to length, insert its bottom end into the mortise and snuggle its top against the underside of the rail, centering it to match its neighbors. (If the tenon is too big, trim it down gradually with a rasp or sandpaper; if it's too small, Raymond wraps a piece of paper around it and glues it in place.) Then dab

Measuring Up: To determine the length of the new baluster (above), Raymond transfers measurements from another baluster that's in the same relative location on a step. After taking additional measurements, he pencils in the location of the future baluster on the underside of the railing.

Stealing the Angle: To find the angle of the top cut, Raymond holds the blade of a bevel gauge (top right) against the bottom of the rail while aligning the tool's body with a nearby baluster. Once the angle is set, it can easily be transferred to the new baluster. To make the cut, Raymond relies on the pinpoint accuracy of a miter saw.

Securing the Spindle: After test fitting the baluster to make sure it fits in with the neighbors, Raymond secures it to the underside of the railing with trim nails (right), angling them towards each other to lock the wood into place. Finally, he sets the nails and fills the holes.

carpenter's glue on the top of the baluster, hold it in place against the hand rail and predrill a couple of holes to keep the wood (especially hardwood) from splitting as you secure it with toenails. Raymond likes to use 2-inch long hardwood trim nails instead of standard finishing nails because they're thinner, harder and coated to reduce woodsplitting. When the baluster is secure, nail on the tread return with 2½-inch hardwood trim nails.

When the job is done, fill the nailheads. Your stairs are suitable for climbing again.

[**curing** the **cold**]

STOP HEATED AIR FROM getting out, and cold air will never get in. Easy enough. But driven by guilt, home owners frequently try one of two solutions to warm up a cold, drafty house. "They go up into the attic and toss around a few batts of fiberglass insulation," says Frazer Dougherty, a home-energy expert in Greenport, New York. "Or they go out and get new windows." Yet neither will guarantee a more comfortable house or even a lower fuel bill.

to find leaks, *moisten your hand with water (to amplify the effect of cold) and hold it close to the edges of windows, doors and other suspect locations. Cold-air creeping in will be easily felt.*

"I just looked at a really big house where the home owners spent $70,000 on new windows," Dougherty says. "But they still go to bed with their hats on." Piecemeal efforts are bound to turn into expensive failures unless they're part of a two-part strategy to tighten up a house from the basement to the roof: Seal gaps, then insulate the right way. Done correctly, this can make any house more comfy, whether it's subjected to long deep-freezes or the occasional cold snap. And, says Dougherty, there's an added benefit: "These very same repairs will help keep hot air out of a house during the summer."

The key to getting control of your indoor climate is understanding how air moves through a house. As warm air rises, it flies out of any available opening, including windows, doors and a long list of seams, cracks and penetrations. Cold air is literally sucked inside through holes and cracks down below to replace the exiting warm air. "One cubic foot of air goes out, one cubic foot of air goes in," says Fred Lugano of Lake Construction in

Vermont. "You have to block that flow." In any house, but particularly those older than a decade or so, there are many places where leaks are common.

The basement figures largely in the infiltration of cold air, even with the door to the upstairs closed tight. Air flowing in through cracks around the sill can be blocked with caulk or expandable foam sealant. Outdoor penetrations for wiring and faucets and the casings around doors and windows should be caulked, as should gaps around pipes and ducts that lead to the first floor.

Vented crawl spaces also pose a problem because they expose the floor to cold air. The floor framing can absorb potentially damaging moisture that rises up from the soil. Treat the floor as if it were over a basement by sealing any penetrations and putting insulation

The familiar batt of fiberglass (left) is the most common household insulation. It's inexpensive, fire-resistant and doesn't settle or disintegrate with age. With an R-value of 3.1 to 4 per inch, it can be be layered as needed. But fiberglass batts don't seal very well and may present potential health hazards. Blown-in fiberglass (right) is of greater concern because fibers are so respirable.

[curingthecold]

any joint
between building materials is a likely place to find air leaking into the house. If two dissimilar materials meet—where siding meets brick, for example—the chances are even greater.

between the joists. To block soil moisture, spread six-mil polyethylene sheeting over the ground and cover it with a layer of sand.

Making a basement tighter is a worthy goal, but it can be overdone. To operate safely, gas- and oil-fired furnaces, boilers and water heaters must have adequate amounts of combustion air. In a tightly sealed basement, they should get it from a nearby louvered window or from a duct that leads from the outside directly to the burner.

When carefully weather-stripped, older double-hung windows can be nearly as tight as new ones. There are several ways to do this but all involve creating a seal around the perimeter of each closed sash. To keep most of the weather stripping out of sight, use thin strips of Q-lon, a slippery nylon-covered foam that makes it easy to slide a sash up and down. Staple Q-lon to the outside edge of the stop for the lower sash and, for the upper sash, to the outside edge of the parting bead. A different product—a plastic V-strip—press-fits into a 2-millimeter-wide groove routed into the meeting rail. To bridge the gap between meeting rail and stop, a bristled self-stick pad with an integral plastic fin seals the jamb at the top of the lower sash. The windows may now be a little harder to open and shut, but they'll be a lot less drafty.

Ceiling penetrations around old pipes and wiring (right) deserve a shot of expanding foam sealant, the button-upper's best friend. Attic hatchways (facing page) call for a different strategy. A box made of rigid, foil-covered insulation board, dogged down with straps, minimizes the heat loss through this normally leaky point. Loosen the straps and the lightweight box moves aside for attic access.

Doors are fairly easy to weather-strip. You can add seals to the existing stops or install new stops fitted with strips of Q-lon. Be careful not to press the strips too tightly into the door; that can make it harder to close. The bottom of a door presents more of a problem. Many sweeps attached to the door's inside ruin the door's looks. But one type, a double-finned sweep made of silicone rubber, is concealed in a groove routed in the door's bottom edge. Once installed, it is easily adjusted to make a tight seal with the threshold.

Although newer versions of recessed lights contain an air-lock system that stops air leaks, older models are little more than heat vents opening directly into the attic. In attics with flat ceilings, one way to retrofit older models is to make a drywall box big enough to leave three inches of clearance between it and the fixture. That's enough space for the fixture to ventilate properly and doesn't create a fire hazard. Once caulked into place, the box can be safely covered with insulation. For recessed lights on sloped ceilings, and in kitchen and lower-floor bathroom soffits—potentially big heat losers—the task is messier. To reach them,

«Piecemeal efforts are bound to turn into expensive failures unless they're part of a two-part strategy to tighten up a house from the basement to the roof: Seal gaps, then insulate the right way. **»**

[curing the cold]

drywall has to be ripped out, after which new insulation can be installed above the old fixture or a more efficient new one.

In an otherwise tight house, knee walls—the short walls that meet sloped ceilings in the top floors of Capes and bungalows and in finished attics—are sometimes a big source of heat loss. Installing insulation between the rafters may seem like the best strategy, but it can leave the space behind a knee wall cold and drafty because batts alone are ineffective air barriers. A continuous sheet of four-mil-thick polyethylene should be stapled to the rafters over the insulation. Caulk the seams along the band joist, or blocking, at the ends

A router plows the groove (left) for an adjustable door sweep that stays out of sight. Blowing-in insulation (facing page) is a dusty job that can dramatically lower fuel bills.

of the floor joists. To cut off another possible draft, install and caulk more blocking between the joists where they pass under the knee wall.

Rising warm air finds its way into the attic through gaps around wiring, ceiling-mounted light fixtures, plumbing vents, ductwork and the chimney. Small gaps can be sealed with expandable foam. Larger ones should be filled with pieces of foam board, cut to shape and caulked in place. But for fire safety, gaps around the chimney should be covered only with sheet metal. Keep any insulation at least two inches away from the chimney.

Although interior partition walls don't require insulation, the tops of these walls can vent tremendous amounts of heat into the attic. If parts of the top plate have been cut away, or if quirky framing has left entire sections without a plate, the opening should be sealed with foam board caulked in place.

As with some partition walls, the stud cavities of balloon-framed exterior walls are sometimes completely open to the attic, which creates wide pathways for heat loss. These should be sealed and caulked at the ceiling joists in the attic.

Attic hatches and ceiling-mounted whole-house fans are the equivalents of large, gaping holes in the top floor. Both can be covered with boxes made of rigid foil-faced foam insulation board, assembled from a kit with foil tape and construction adhesive. Weather stripping lines the bottom edges, and Velcro straps pull the boxes tight to the attic floor. After the house is sealed, it's time to take a hard look at its insulation.

* * *

TYPES OF INSULATION

ADDING EXTRA INSULATION CAN CONTRIBUTE MUCH TO A HOUSE'S overall comfort, but it's the final step and should be taken only after doing as much air-sealing as is practical. "Installing insulation before you seal is only going to hide your problems, not solve them," says Lugano. In colder climates, insulating the ceiling of an unheated basement is a good idea. Even though warm air rises, heat also radiates down through the floorboards. Here, fiberglass batts are useful because they fit easily around obstructions.

[curing**the**cold]

Ducts, plumbing runs and wiring commonly run through the joist bays. Batts can be held in place with wooden lath or plastic strips but should never be compressed. That diminishes their R-value. Not everyone needs to insulate the floor, however. "In Arkansas, and southern states in general, it's just not cost effective," says Royce Lewis of Comfort Diagnostics and Solutions in Little Rock. "The money can be better spent making other parts of the house tighter."

The best type of insulation for attics, Lugano says, is not fiberglass but cellulose or cotton, made by shredding old newsprint or fabric. To attain its full insulation value, either type must be unloaded from sacks into a special machine, which can be rented, that fluffs it up and pumps it through a four-inch hose into the attic. Some say that six inches of insulation is enough, but Lugano prefers a full foot in Vermont. And the same is true in warmer climates. "We go for twelve inches of cellulose minimum," says Lewis. "It takes at least that much to stop the sun from heating through the insulation in the summer."

Another attic improvement that will help to contain heat year-round is a radiant barrier. The barrier isn't thick insulation but rather a thin reflective sheet that comes in long, wide rolls. Stapled over the rafters, it reflects heat radiating from the backside of the roof, a considerable source of unwanted heat gain during the warmest months. That's its main benefit, but the reflective side facing the attic also slows heat loss during the cooler months. "Combined with traditional insulation," says Philip Fairey of the Florida Solar Energy Center, "it gives you extra energy savings."

keeping warm, staying healthy

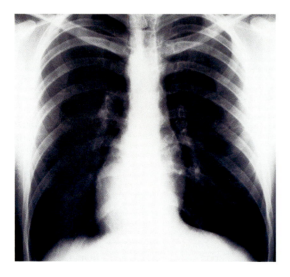

SOMETIMES IT SEEMS AS IF HOMES ARE FULL OF DANGERS. THERE IS LEAD IN PAINT, RADON IN BASEMENTS AND FORMALDEHYDE IN CARPETS. IS FIBERGLASS INSULATION A PROBLEM, TOO? THE DEBATE CAME TO A HEAD IN 1993, WHEN A FEDERAL AGENCY LISTED FIBERGLASS AS A POSSIBLE CARCINOGEN. VARIOUS STUDIES FOLLOWED: SOME SUPPORTED THIS CONCLUSION, SOME DEBUNKED IT. HOME OWNERS, OF COURSE, WONDER WHAT IT ALL MEANS.

IF FIBERGLASS FIBERS STAYED PUT ONCE INSTALLED, THERE MIGHT BE LITTLE CONCERN. BUT THE FIBERS OFTEN DON'T SIT UNDISTURBED. FAMILY MEMBERS TRAMP IN AND OUT OF FIBERGLASS-FILLED ATTICS. AND IN HOMES THAT HAVE FORCED-AIR HEATING SYSTEMS, DUCTS SURROUNDED BY FIBERGLASS CAN LEAK, ALLOWING SMALL BITS TO BE DRAWN INTO THE RETURNS, SUCKED THROUGH THE FURNACE FILTER AND BLOWN INTO THE HOUSE. IN THE ABSENCE OF DEFINITIVE INFORMATION, BE PRUDENT. WEAR A RESPIRATOR WHEN INSTALLING OR REMOVING FIBERGLASS. MINIMIZE DISRUPTION OF THE MATERIAL. AND CONSIDER THE ALTERNATIVES.

POLYICYNENE FOAM:
Made of modified ure-
thane, a plastic similar to
that in mattress foams.
Sprayed into walls and
attics with water as a
blowing agent. Pros: Sta-
bilizes wobbly plaster.
Seals gaps. Almost imper-
meable to moisture and
air. Cons: Expensive.
R-value: 3.6 per inch.

**POLYISOCYANURATE FOAM
BOARD:** Rigid plastic foam
for roofs and walls. Blowing agent is the same as
that used in extruded
polystyrene. Pros: Mois-
ture-resistant. R-value: 6.6
to 7 per inch.

CELLULOSE: Made of mostly
recycled shredded paper plus
boric acid or other fire retardant. Sprayed dry, dampened
with acrylic binder or wet into
attics or walls. Pros: While
blown-in fiberglass' R-value
can decrease considerably
when temperature outside is
70-76 degrees colder than
inside, the R-value of cellulose
is unaffected. Cons: Can settle
if sprayed dry. Extremely dusty
during installation. R-value: 3.7
to 3.8 per inch.

CEMENTITIOUS FOAM: Made
of magnesium compounds
extracted from seawater.
Sprayed into wall cavities. Pros:
Fireproof. Cons: Can crumble;
needs surface protection. Not
good for earthquake country.
Expensive. R-value: 3.9 per inch.

**EXPANDED POLYSTYRENE FOAM
BOARD:** Made of petroleum by-
product; up to half can be recycled polystyrene. Pros: Blowing
agent does not deplete ozone.
Good for narrow places. Impermeable to moisture. Cons: Expensive. R-value: 3.9 per inch.

COTTON: Shredded scraps
of blue denim, plus poly-
ester binder and a flame
retardant. Comes in batts
and loose fibers. Pros:
Absorbs less moisture
than cellulose (but more
than fiberglass).
Cons: Check local codes
for approval. R-value: 3.1
to 3.3 per inch.

**EXTRUDED POLYSTYRENE
FOAM BOARD:** Same plas-
tic as expanded poly-
styrene. Pros: Good for
sheathing. Impermeable to
moisture. Cons: Expen-
sive. Uses a slightly
ozone-depleting blowing
agent. R-value: 5 per inch.

POLYURETHANE FOAM: A
sprayed-in-place plastic
for walls, attics and roofs.
Pros: Seals gaps. Almost
impermeable to moisture
and air movement. Cons:
Blowing agent may be
ozone-depleting. Can't be
used in existing walls
unless wall surface is
removed. R-value: 6.7 to
7.3 per inch.

[freezeproofing]

An outdoor faucet

serves up a steady, endless stream of water

RIGHT WHERE IT'S NEEDED, ALL SUMMER LONG. BUT WINTER CAN TURN this amenity into a nuisance, or worse. "The exciting day isn't the day it freezes," says Richard Trethewey. "It's the day it thaws, and you have a hydrant blowing water into your basement." That's due to a design of many faucets that leaves them highly vulnerable to plummeting temperatures.

The problem is common to houses more than about 10 years old, and stems from the location of the faucet's washer, just below the faucet handle. When the faucet is turned off, water stops at the washer and is trapped within the spigot itself, in the worst possible place for it in cold weather: outside the walls. If the spigot hasn't been drained before the first freeze—quite common, says Richard, because home owners like to keep these handy taps going—the water inside (and in the pipe leading to it) can turn to ice. The ice expands,

pressure builds up and the weakest element of the system, the pipe, bursts. Now that wonderfully handy stream of water, the one that filled the pool and greened-up the lawn all summer, is pouring directly into your walls. Maybe you'll hear the water rushing; maybe you'll even remember where the shut-off is (and hopefully you'll have one). But it's just as likely that you'll be away from the house for the day or, worse, on vacation. That's when a nuisance turns into a catastrophe.

In contrast, the washer of a freeze-proof

A Tale of Two Faucets: On a traditional spigot (1), the washer is next to the faucet handle, outside of the house and exposed to the cold weather. On a freeze-proof faucet, the washer is at the end of an internal stem (2) that slides into an external stem (3); it ends up 6-inches or more inside the house, protected from the elements.

1

Washer

Internal stem

2

Washer

3

External stem

ALL THREE OF THE VALVES BELOW SHUT OFF WATER, MAKING IT EASIER TO REPAIR AN OUTDOOR FAUCET. IF THERE'S NO SHUTOFF, ADD ONE WHEN REPLACING THE FAUCET. MANY PROFESSIONALS PREFER THE TYPE IN THE MIDDLE, SAYS RICHARD TRETHEWEY. A STOP VALVE (LEFT) SEALS WITH A WASHER THAT MUST EVENTUALLY BE REPLACED. A GATE VALVE (RIGHT) WORKS BY WAY OF A METAL-TO-METAL SEAL; ELECTROLYSIS, HOWEVER, CAN CAUSE IT TO FAIL. IN A BALL VALVE (MIDDLE), A STAINLESS STEEL BALL PRESSES AGAINST TEFLON OR RUBBER, CREATING A LONG-LASTING, DRIP-PROOF SEAL.

open and shut

the pipe

connecting an outdoor faucet to a water supply sometimes passes through an oversize hole that lets insects and cold air into the house. Seal the hole with silicone caulk.

faucet is 6 inches or more inside the house, within the protective envelope of the walls. When the faucet is turned off, all the water between the washer and the spigot itself drains out the stem automatically. With no water, there's no water to freeze.

A freeze-proof faucet costs only about $20 and takes an hour or so to install. "You'll never think about your outdoor faucets again," says Richard. "And hey, there's always that one warm day in February when you might want to wash the car."

AVOIDING BURST PIPES

Old-style spigots aren't the only source of water damage caused by cold weather. In the past decade or so, insurance companies have paid home owners $4 billion for damage caused by frozen and ruptured pipes. The worst problem, surprisingly, is in warmer

②

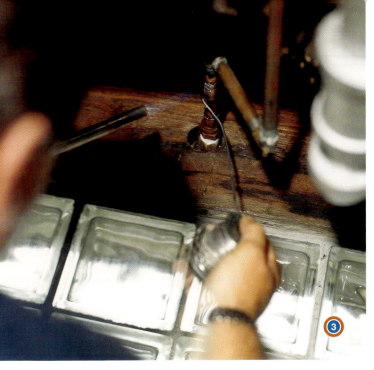

③

climates, according to Jeff Gordon of the Building Research Center in Champaign, Illinois. He suggests several tips for avoiding such costly aggravation.

Well before the first freeze, turn off the valve that feeds non-freezeproof outdoor faucets, then open the faucet and let it drain. That prevents water from collecting inside the faucet. If your house is not equipped with shut-off valves—many older houses aren't, or don't have enough of them—this would be a good time to add them.

To prevent garden hoses from rupturing, drain them and store them where temperatures won't drop below freezing. Drain all in-ground sprinkler systems, too, and don't forget to drain any portable watering devices such as oscillating sprinklers and trigger-sprayers.

And if the house will remain unoccupied for a few weeks during winter, be sure to leave the thermostat set at 55 degrees Fahrenheit. Even freeze-proof faucets won't help much if frigid weather invades the house and ruptures unprotected pipes.

TECHNIQUES

A **Faucet Departs:** Before removing the old faucet, Richard Trethewey shut off its water supply, drained the spigot and cut the pipe close to where the new connection would be. The hole for the old faucet was too big for the new one, so carpenter Charlie Silva (1) patched in a small piece of wood flush with the siding and used a right-angle drill to make the new hole.

I **nserting a New Stem:** Richard (2) guides the faucet, pipe and plastic flange into the hole Silva drilled, then snugs up the screws so the spigot is securely fastened to the house. "You will often need a fitting to make some adjustment," says Richard. The new pipe was short by $2\frac{1}{2}$ inches, so he cut a piece of $\frac{1}{2}$-inch copper pipe—in this case, a piece from the old faucet worked fine—and extended the shaft to the proper length.

C **onnecting the Pipes:** Inside the house, Richard checks the fit of the new pipes, cleans the end of each one with emery cloth, and applies solder flux before firing up his torch. When the pipes are heated (3), the flux acts as a catalyst between solder and copper, ensuring a solid connection. Soldering completed, Richard turns the water back on in the basement and checks for leaks.

[**weather**stripping]

STEVE AND HILARY CHASIN LOVE THEIR 62-YEAR-OLD SLATE-ROOFED Georgian on Long Island and its windows—43 double-hung, single-glazed eyes looking out on wide sycamore-lined streets. But from the day they moved in, they realized that all 43 windows let cold air get into the house. "We had to keep the thermostat at 80 degrees just to feel comfortable," says Hilary.

the best
weather stripping to use depends on the type of window and the skill of the installer. Various types and materials are available (see below). All depend on a compression fit.

Determined to fix the problem but reluctant to part with the handblown glass in every sash, the couple turned to window restoration contractor John Stahl. "The simple fact is that only 10 percent of heat is lost through the glass in a window," he says. "The rest is lost from the perimeter." Stahl's solution for the Chasins' windows: Rout grooves around three sides of each sash and slide in soft, fuzzy weather stripping. Similar to the weather stripping found on automobile windows, the nylon pile seals gaps as wide as ¼ inch. Although the trim holding a sash in place must be removed carefully, Stahl says almost anyone can install this type of weather stripping. And the real bonus: Weather-stripping materials cost a lot less than replacement windows.

While the frame is opened up, Stahl grabs the chance to check the window's hardware. He recommends replacing aging cotton sash cords with high-quality braided nylon rope. Old chains can be swapped for bronze, copper or galvanized steel. Check to make sure pulleys spin freely. If they resist, scrape off excess paint, or drop them in a bucket of paint remover, then apply household oil. If all else fails, replace them.

To reinstall a sash, Stahl holds it in place and checks to see if it fits snugly from side to side and moves easily up and down. If it's too tight, he planes off some wood; if it's too loose, he removes the weather stripping and slips thicker stuff into place. Then he rehangs each sash and installs new stops.

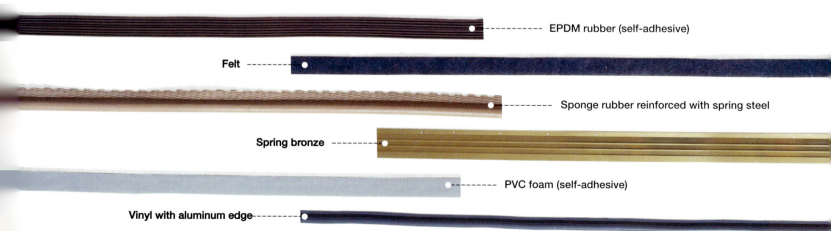

EPDM rubber (self-adhesive)

Felt

Sponge rubber reinforced with spring steel

Spring bronze

PVC foam (self-adhesive)

Vinyl with aluminum edge

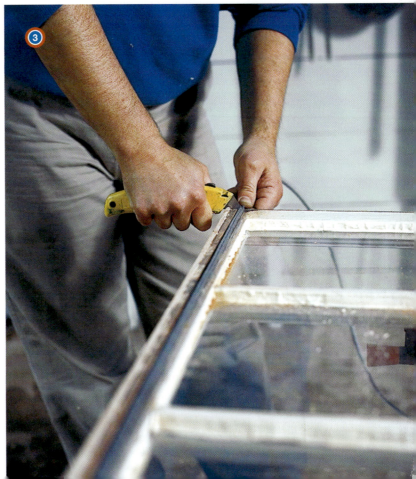

Removing the Sash: Before Stahl pulls out the sash (1), he breaks any paint seals with a utility knife, prys off the stops and cuts the sash cords, letting the sash weights fall. (He'll retrieve them later by removing access panels on either side of the window.)

Cutting a Channel: Using a router (2) with a three-wing slot cutting bit, Stahl cuts a ⅛-inch wide by ⅜-inch deep channel around three outer edges of the sash, excluding the meeting rail edge. Because two of the edges house the sash cord, he's careful to avoid the existing grooves.

Installing the Weather Stripping: After routing a groove on the lower sash's meeting rail, Stahl slides ⅛-inch pile weather stripping into place (3) and fits more weather stripping into the grooves he cut earlier.

[servicing a switch]

HIDDEN BEHIND A WALL IN VIRTUALLY EVERY ROOM IN A HOUSE LIES one of the simplest yet most graceful of electrical devices. There, inside a tiny plastic case, wires lead to two metal contacts that open or close—turning a nearby light fixture off or on with the touch of a human hand. Such an overlooked device. The basic mechanics of a light switch have changed little in a hundred years. Invented in the early 1880s, early switches had rotary or push-button actuators that produced a loud snap when turned or pushed.

electricians *warn against using inexpensive switches with push-in (versus screw-in) terminals for wires. The wires can work their way out, leaving an open circuit.*

This waterproof switch has sealed seams and a foam gasket to keep its innards dry; it could be used outside a back door.

Push-button switches are still found in turn-of-the-century houses. (Indeed, the crew of *This Old House* found push-button switches throughout the Victorian house they renovated in Watertown, Massachusetts.)

In the 1920s, switches with a toggle actuator became standard, and they remain one of the great bargains at hardware stores: an item that costs less than about $3 is quite likely to last 50 years. Since the 1980s, switches with flat paddles, or rockers, have been gaining acceptance.

What has changed most over the years is not the switch mechanism itself, but the variety of options. There are switches with timers, dimmers, glowing toggles and motion sensors. Even more options exist for the wall plate, which is sold separately from the switch. Unaffected by all the hoopla on the surface, the mechanism inside a switch continues to light up a room the way it always has: safely, dependably, immediately.

The most common mistake that home owners make when changing a switch, says *This Old House* electrician Allen Gallant, is failing to properly ground the new one. "Look for the green grounding screw on the yoke," he says, "and attach the grounding conductor from the box to that screw. That grounding conductor is the most important wire in the whole circuit." Gallant says home owners often overlook this step because the old switch being removed might not have a grounding screw—an innovation that didn't become standard until about 1970.

Three-way switches are often replaced incorrectly, too, says Gallant. "The key is making sure the wire that was on the old switch's common terminal screw is wired to the new switch's common terminal screw."

As simple as a switch is, however, don't work on one unless you've taken a crucial precaution: Turn off the electricity first.

behind the plate

Ampere and volt capacity are stamped into yoke.

ALL SWITCHES ARE RATED FOR AMPERAGE AS WELL AS CURRENT-CARRYING CAPACITY. A STANDARD RESIDENTIAL SWITCH IS RATED AT 15 AMPS AND 120 VOLTS—SUFFICIENT FOR ALMOST ANY LIGHTING APPLICATION AROUND THE HOUSE.

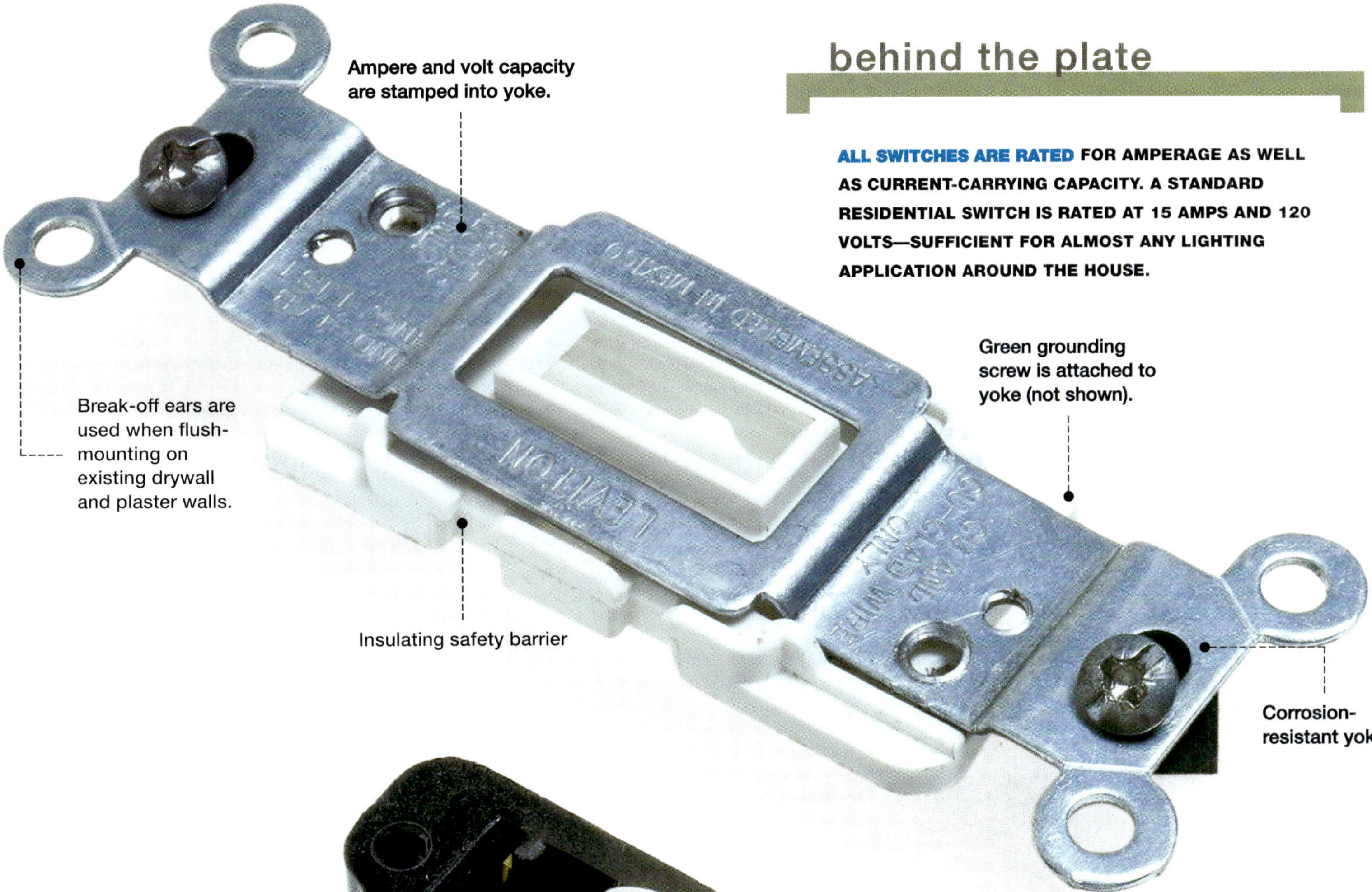

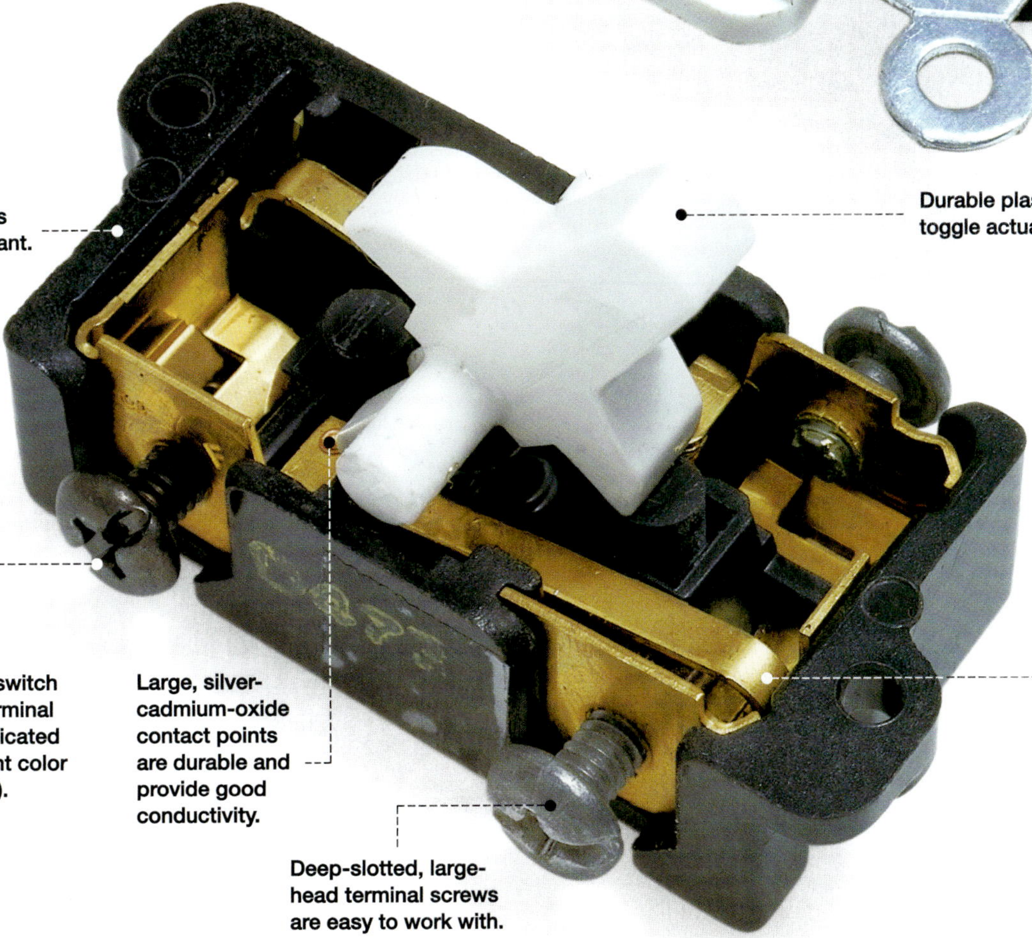

Break-off ears are used when flush-mounting on existing drywall and plaster walls.

Green grounding screw is attached to yoke (not shown).

Insulating safety barrier

Corrosion-resistant yoke

Thermoplastic case is strong and arc-resistant.

Durable plastic toggle actuator

Three-way-switch common terminal screw is indicated by a different color (here, black).

Large, silver-cadmium-oxide contact points are durable and provide good conductivity.

Deep-slotted, large-head terminal screws are easy to work with.

One-piece copper-alloy contact arm offers quiet, firm action and good conductivity.

* * *
CREDITS

AUTHORS: Alexandra Bandon, Patricia E. Berry, Don Best, Joe Carter, Joseph D'Agnese, Brooke Deterline, Mark Feirer, Jeanne Huber, Peter Jensen, Ben Kalin, Sasha Nyary, Stephen L. Petranek, Hope Reeves, Curtis Rist, Laurence Roy Stains, Wendy Talarico and Logan Ward.

PHOTOGRAPHERS: Bernd Auers, FPG International, Noah Greenberg, Michael Grimm, Darrin Haddad, Spencer Jones, Keller & Keller, Michael McLaughlin, Michael Myers, Benjamin Oliver, Rosa & Rosa, Jason Schmidt, Kolin Smith and Adam Weiss. Microfiber photographs courtesy of Thomas Hopen/MVA Incorporated.

ILLUSTRATIONS: Bob Hambly, Pierre Le-Tan and Steven Stankiewicz.

THIS OLD HOUSE® BOOKS
EDITOR: Mark Feirer
CREATIVE DIRECTOR: Matthew Drace
ART DIRECTOR: Dina White
ART ASSOCIATE: Matthew Bates
PRODUCTION ASSOCIATE: Duane Stapp
COPY EDITOR: Terrie Piell

DIRECTOR, NEW PRODUCT DEVELOPMENT: Bob Fox
ASSISTANT PRODUCT MANAGER: Miriam Silver

SPECIAL THANKS TO: Norm Abram, Steve Thomas, Tom Silva, Richard Trethewey, Bruce Irving and Russell Morash at the show; Betsy Groban and Peter McGhee at WGBH; Stephen VanHove and Anthony Wendling at Applied Graphics Technology; Robert Hardin; Chris "Scanman" Kwieraga and Michele "Photofinder" Fleury at *This Old House* magazine.

Funding for *This Old House* on public television is provided by State Farm Insurance Companies, Ace Hardware Corporation and The Minwax & Krylon Brands.

« Old buildings are like people. If you know how to listen, they will tell you how they are feeling. **»**